Other Books by Roxie Kelley

*At Our Table*

*Goodness Gracious*

*Keeping Good Company*

*With Heart and Soul*

*Just a Matter of Thyme*

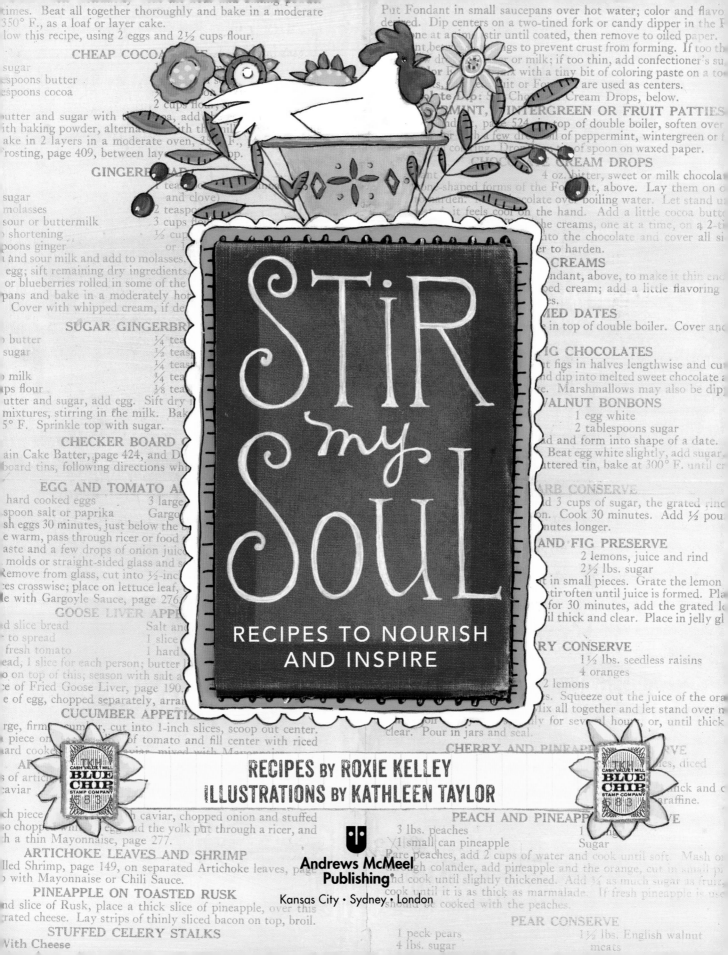

# Stir my Soul

## RECIPES TO NOURISH AND INSPIRE

RECIPES BY ROXIE KELLEY
ILLUSTRATIONS BY KATHLEEN TAYLOR

Andrews McMeel
Publishing

Kansas City · Sydney · London

Andrews McMeel Publishing, LLC
an Andrews McMeel Universal company
1130 Walnut Street, Kansas City, Missouri 64106

www.andrewsmcmeel.com

14 15 16 17 18 SHO 10 9 8 7 6 5 4 3 2 1

ISBN: 978-1-4494-2737-5

Library of Congress Control Number: 2012940550

ATTENTION: SCHOOLS AND BUSINESSES
Andrews McMeel books are available at quantity discounts with bulk purchase for educational, business, or sales promotional use. For information, please e-mail the Andrews McMeel Publishing Special Sales Department: specialsales@amuniversal.com

To Jerry Huisenga,
my father who became my friend.
With love,
Roxie

To my parents, who gave me art lessons and encouragement;
and FDA, who believes I can do anything.
With love and gratitude,
Kathleen

Vacancy

# CONTENTS

Hello Again, My Friends!
xii

## appetizers

# Main Dishes

# Side dishes and salads

# breads

# desserts

# this and that

# HELLO AGAIN, MY FRIENDS!

I'm so excited to be able to share *Stir My Soul* with you.

After writing several cookbooks, I began to notice that the words used to describe the actions required in cooking—stirring, folding, measuring, blending—were the same words and actions that describe my daily living. My friends and family were part of my "fold," and I found myself "measuring" my words when I spoke to my children . . . you see where this is headed. Because I love words, I found a certain pleasure in that realization, and I wanted to share it with you. A coming to terms with terms, if you will.

All the steaming, stewing, tenderizing, and even the aging in the course of my life, had, like good recipes, led to a satisfying result—a "becoming," like a completed favorite dish or dessert. There are times in life when compartmentalizing is helpful. But sometimes it's good to see how all of our ordinary moments blend together to make an extraordinary life.

And so, this book is a compilation of some fabulous and faithful recipes with some thoughts on not just what we are doing with our actions but also who we are becoming in the process. Life is, after all, not only about the list of actions we undertake in the recipe of our days. It is about the people we are becoming and the flavor we add to the lives of those around us.

And speaking of adding flavor: Sharing her incredible and flavorful art with you is Kathleen Taylor, whose work I've admired and enjoyed for years. Kathleen's art is featured prominently in our restaurant, the Paint Box Café, and I often wish I could record our customers' comments and play them back to her. Her work always produces smiles, and collecting it is definitely habit-forming.

We both thank you for the privilege of sharing our process of "becoming" with you and sincerely hope these pages will stir your soul.

My Best to You,

Roxie Kelley

APPETIZERS

# Spinach Artichoke Nachos

This appetizer comes together very quickly. I like the idea of using fresh rather than frozen spinach, as is seen in most spinach artichoke dip recipes. This is especially beautiful when served on a large platter.

### SERVES 6 TO 8

2 tablespoons unsalted butter

2 teaspoons minced garlic

1 (5-ounce) package fresh baby spinach, chopped

⅓ cup cream

1 cup shaved Parmesan cheese

1 teaspoon Worcestershire sauce

1 teaspoon freshly squeezed lemon juice

Salt and freshly ground black pepper

1 (14-ounce) can artichoke hearts, drained and chopped

1 (7-ounce) bag multigrain tortilla chips

1 (6-ounce) package shredded mozzarella cheese

2 cups salsa of your choice

Preheat the oven to 425°F. In a medium pan, melt the butter over medium-low heat. Cook the garlic in the butter for 30 seconds. Add the spinach, cream, Parmesan cheese, Worcestershire, lemon juice, and salt and pepper to taste. Stir to combine and cook until wilted, about 1 minute. Stir in the artichoke hearts.

Scatter the tortilla chips on a large ovenproof platter or baking sheet. Spoon the spinach mixture evenly over the chips. Sprinkle with the mozzarella. Bake for 8 to 10 minutes, until the cheese is bubbly. Serve warm with the salsa on the side.

# Miniature Meatballs

I've served these meatballs at several parties in the past few years. I like preparing them a day or two in advance to minimize the number of last-minute preparations required in entertaining.

### SERVES 8 TO 10

2 pounds ground beef chuck

2 large eggs, beaten

1 cup dry bread crumbs

1 (1-ounce) package dried onion soup mix

1 (16-ounce) can whole-berry cranberry sauce

1 cup ketchup

1 cup firmly packed light brown sugar

1 (16-ounce) can sauerkraut, rinsed and drained

1 cup water

Preheat the oven to 350°F. Combine the beef, eggs, bread crumbs, and soup mix in a large bowl. Form into meatballs using approximately 2 tablespoons of the mixture for each. Arrange in a single layer in a 13 by 9-inch baking dish.

Combine the cranberry sauce, ketchup, brown sugar, sauerkraut, and water in a medium bowl. Mix well. Pour the sauce over the meatballs. Bake until bubbling, about 1 hour. Serve hot.

# Brooke's Sweet Potato Hummus

This is my daughter's recipe. The first year Brooke lived away from home, we decided to create a traveling journal together. The journal was our "across the miles" way of sharing the little projects and experiences that we used to do together when she was still at home. If there was a cooking experiment or an art idea, it went lovingly into the journal and then into a flat rate postage box. Three days later, we felt the tug of the heartstrings and got a dose of inspiration as a bonus. So when you taste this hummus or Brooke's Crisp Banana Waffles (page 89), imagine the traveling journal, overstuffed with photos, collages, recipes, and love, making its way from Missouri to California and back again. Joy in a box.

1 sweet potato, peeled and cut into ½-inch cubes

1 (15.5-ounce) can chickpeas, rinsed and drained

¼ cup freshly squeezed lemon juice

¼ cup tahini

3 tablespoons olive oil

2 teaspoons ground cumin

1 clove garlic, minced

Salt and freshly ground black pepper

Assorted fresh vegetables or toasted
pita bread, for serving

Place the sweet potato in a bowl and add just enough water to cover the potato pieces. Loosely cover the bowl with a damp paper towel and microwave on high power for 5 to 6 minutes, until tender. Drain and transfer the sweet potato to the bowl of a food processor fitted with a chopping blade. Add the chickpeas, lemon juice, tahini, olive oil, cumin, and garlic. Pulse until the mixture is smooth and creamy. Add a little more olive oil to thin if necessary and pulse again. Season with salt and pepper to taste. Cover and refrigerate until ready to serve. Serve with fresh vegetables or toasted pita bread.

# Greek Nachos

This recipe reminds me of a party our friends hosted after they returned from Greece. Every item on the menu was a dish they had enjoyed while vacationing there. What a fun way for us to share in their experience and to allow them to revisit the scrumptious foods they missed after the trip was over. This tzatziki sauce makes 2 cups, so you will have some left over for use in a gyro or on a sandwich.

## SERVES 4 TO 6

### TZATZIKI SAUCE

1 (8-ounce) container plain yogurt

1 cucumber, peeled, seeded, and diced

1 tablespoon olive oil

¼ cup freshly squeezed lemon juice

Salt and freshly ground black pepper

1 teaspoon fresh dill

1 teaspoon minced garlic

### NACHOS

1 (9-ounce) bag pita chips

1 (10-ounce) container hummus

1 cucumber, diced

1 tomato, diced

1 cup crumbled feta cheese

¼ cup diced red onion

To make the tzatziki sauce, in a food processor, combine the yogurt, cucumber, olive oil, lemon juice, salt, pepper, dill, and garlic. Process until well combined. Divide the sauce between two containers. Cover and refrigerate for at least 1 hour before serving.

To assemble the nachos, on a large platter, layer the pita chips, hummus, cucumber, tomato, feta cheese, red onion, and tzatziki sauce. Serve at room temperature.

# Cheesy Cracker BREAD

This is a very nice complement to a salad, and it is also delicious served as an appetizer with hummus or thin slices of salami.

## MAKES SIX 8-INCH ROUNDS

1 cup all-purpose flour

8 ounces cheddar cheese, shredded

5 tablespoons salted butter, at room temperature

1 tablespoon Worcestershire sauce

⅛ teaspoon cayenne pepper

Sea salt and freshly ground black pepper

In a small bowl, stir together the flour and cheese. In a large bowl, using an electric mixer on low speed, beat together the butter, Worcestershire, and cayenne until blended. Add the flour mixture and beat on medium speed for 1 minute.

On a lightly floured surface, divide the dough into 6 separate pieces, pressing each piece into a flat disk. Wrap each piece in plastic wrap and refrigerate for about 30 minutes.

Preheat the oven to 375°F. On a lightly floured surface, roll each disk into an 8-inch circle. Transfer the circles to baking sheets, leaving about an inch between circles. Sprinkle each circle of dough with salt and pepper to taste. Bake, one sheet at a time, for 10 to 12 minutes, until the edges are lightly golden brown. Cool on the baking sheets for 5 minutes before transferring to a rack to cool completely.

The cracker bread can be stored in an airtight container, separated by layers of waxed paper, at room temperature for up to 3 days.

# Classic Potato Skins

Here is a better way to enjoy potato skins. They are lower in calories, fat, and guilt than the traditional skins. This is the kind of appetizer you can prepare ahead of time (even a day or two in advance), and then just slide into the oven about 10 minutes before you plan to serve your guests.

**SERVES 8 TO 10**

6 Yukon gold potatoes, scrubbed and pierced with a knife

Olive oil cooking spray

Sea salt

3 tablespoons sour cream

¾ cup shredded mozzarella cheese

4 slices prosciutto, cut into small pieces

3 tablespoons chopped fresh chives

Preheat the oven to 425°F. Spray the whole surface of the potatoes with olive oil cooking spray and place in a baking dish. Then lightly coat the surface of each potato with sea salt. Bake uncovered for 1 hour. Remove the dish from the oven and wait a few minutes for the potatoes to cool enough to be handled.

Cut each potato in half lengthwise. With a tablespoon, scoop out the flesh into a medium bowl, leaving the skin intact. Place the skins back into the baking dish. Add the sour cream and cheese to the potatoes in the bowl and mix well with a fork. Spoon this mixture back into the reserved skins and top with the prosciutto. At this time, you may cover the potato skins, refrigerate, and bake later. Or you may return the skins to the oven and bake uncovered for 8 to 10 minutes, until heated through and the cheese is melted. Garnish with the chives and serve.

# Everything Pretzel Bites

Everything luscious in one bite—soft, chewy, salty, savory. If you haven't had much experience with recipes that call for yeast, a good way to judge the temperature for the water in the recipe is to think about how warm you would make the bath water for a toddler.

**SERVES 8 TO 10**

### DOUGH

1½ cups warm water

2 (.25-ounce) packages quick-rise yeast
(2 scant tablespoons)

2 tablespoons light brown sugar

1 teaspoon salt

1 cup bread flour

3 to 4 cups all-purpose flour, plus some for rolling out

### TOPPING INGREDIENTS

2 tablespoons sea salt

2 tablespoons poppy seeds

2 tablespoons sesame seeds

1 tablespoon dehydrated onions

2 tablespoons baking soda

2 cups warm water

4 tablespoons salted butter, melted

To make the dough, pour the warm water into a medium mixing bowl and add the yeast, brown sugar, salt, bread flour, and 1 cup of the all-purpose flour. Mix well. Gradually add the remaining 2 to 3 cups of all-purpose flour and knead until no longer sticky. Cover lightly with plastic wrap and let rest for 20 minutes.

Combine the sea salt, poppy seeds, sesame seeds, and dehydrated onions in a small bowl and set aside.

Preheat the oven to 450°F. Coat two baking sheets with nonstick cooking spray. Turn the dough out onto a lightly floured surface. Roll the dough out to a ¼-inch thickness. With a dough scraper, cut the dough into 1-inch square pieces.

Combine the baking soda and the 2 cups warm water in a large bowl. Dip each piece of dough into the baking soda bath, shaking off the extra water. Then place the dough on a prepared baking sheet. Sprinkle all the pieces with the topping mixture. Bake for 4 to 6 minutes, until golden brown. Brush the melted butter over the pretzels and serve.

# Caramelized Onion and Goat Cheese Tartlets

These make oh-so-amazing appetizers but are also a wonderful choice for brunch. To save time, you can make the filling and cut out the pastry the day before (cover with plastic wrap and store in the refrigerator to keep the pastry from drying out). Try serving them with Canopy Salad (page 61). I use silicone tart molds for this recipe, but you could use the metal type with removable bottoms if you like.

**MAKES 18 TARTLETS**

3 tablespoons olive oil

2 yellow onions, chopped

3 cloves garlic, minced

1 russet potato, peeled and finely chopped

8 ounces goat cheese, crumbled

3 tablespoons chopped fresh chives

8 large eggs, lightly beaten

2 tablespoons half-and-half

Salt and freshly ground black pepper

All-purpose flour, for rolling

1 (17.3-ounce) package puff pastry,
thawed according to package directions

In a medium skillet, heat the oil and add the onions, garlic, and potato. Over medium-low heat, sauté this mixture, about 5 minutes, stirring often, until the onions are softened and caramelized and the potato is golden brown. Let cool.

In a medium bowl, combine the cooled onion mixture with the goat cheese, chives, eggs, half-and-half, and salt and pepper.

On a lightly floured surface, roll out the puff pastry to a ⅛-inch thickness. Cut out 5-inch circles and place each circle in the tart pans or molds, pressing along the edges. Trim the excess along the top with a sharp knife. Prick the bottom of each tart shell several times with a fork.

Evenly distribute the egg filling into each tart. I use a small soup ladle to do this. Refrigerate for 15 minutes and preheat the oven to 425°F.

Bake for 15 to 17 minutes, until the filling is set and the pastry is golden brown around the edges. Cool for 5 minutes before serving.

CHEESe

I have so much respect for Mike and Cheryl Castle, owners of
On the Rise Bakery and Bistro in Osage Beach, Missouri. Not only
do they own and operate one of the finest eating establishments in the
lake area but they are also just wonderful human beings. This recipe
is from Mike. He shares two of his favorite sauces for chicken wings;
each sauce makes enough to coat the 4 pounds of wings. Dig in!

### MAKES ABOUT 4 DOZEN WINGS

Vegetable oil, for frying

4 pounds chicken wings, rinsed and patted dry

Kahlúa and Coffee Sauce (recipe follows) or
Raspberry-Tequila Sauce (recipe follows)

Heat 3 inches of oil in a deep fryer to 350°F. Preheat the oven to
425°F.

Remove the tip from each chicken wing and discard. Cut each
wing in half at the joint.

Fry the chicken wings in batches for 6 to 9 minutes, until crispy
and golden brown and the wings float to the top. Remove from
the oil with a slotted spoon and drain on paper towels.

Place the cooked wings in a large bowl and toss with the sauce
of your choice. Transfer the sauced wings to a heavy baking
sheet. Bake for 4 to 5 minutes to caramelize the sauce. Serve hot.

# Kahlúa & Coffee Sauce

1 tablespoon olive oil

2 tablespoons minced garlic

1 cup ketchup

1 cup aged balsamic vinegar

½ cup freshly squeezed orange juice

½ cup honey

½ cup Kahlúa

½ cup brewed espresso

1 tablespoon prepared horseradish

In a large frying pan, heat the olive oil over medium heat. Sauté the garlic in the olive oil for a minute or two, then add the remaining ingredients and simmer on low heat for 1 hour.

# Raspberry-Tequila Sauce

4 cups purchased raspberry melba sauce

¾ cup gold tequila

½ cup freshly squeezed Key lime juice

1 tablespoon minced fresh cilantro

½ teaspoon salt

Simmer all the ingredients in a heavy saucepan over low heat, stirring constantly until thickened, about 10 minutes.

# French Onion Dip

Even though there is absolutely nothing wrong with the onion dip you find in the dairy case at your grocery store, this version is really worth the 20 minutes you'll spend pulling it together. It tastes so fresh and the rosemary adds a hint of interest you won't find in the premade dips. Serve it with fresh vegetables or your favorite chips.

**MAKES ABOUT 5 CUPS**

2 tablespoons unsalted butter

2 sweet onions, sliced
¼ inch thick

2 teaspoons minced garlic

1 tablespoon chopped
fresh rosemary

2 cups sour cream

1 cup mayonnaise

1 teaspoon celery salt

1 teaspoon Worcestershire sauce

Salt and freshly ground
black pepper

Potato chips, for serving

In a large skillet, melt the butter over medium-high heat. Add the onions and sauté, stirring occasionally, for 8 to 10 minutes, until golden brown and caramelized. Add the garlic and sauté for an additional minute. Remove from the heat and stir in the rosemary. Transfer the mixture to a plastic cutting board to cool.

In a large bowl, combine the sour cream, mayonnaise, celery salt, Worcestershire, and salt and pepper to taste. Chop the onion mixture into small pieces, and when completely cool, fold into the sour cream mixture. Refrigerate for at least 1 hour—overnight is even better. Serve with potato chips.

# Kelly's Barbecue Mushroom Bites

Thanks to Kelly Garr for sharing this yummy appetizer idea. Kelly prepares these on the grill, but I've adapted them here for baking in the oven. At a recent engagement party for one of my son's friends, these little tidbits were the first to "sell out"—definitely the star appetizer of the evening.

**SERVES 6**

12 slices bacon, cut in half

1 (8-ounce) container fresh
Monterey button mushrooms (24 mushrooms)

1 cup sweet barbecue sauce of your choice

Preheat the oven to 450°F. Line a baking pan with aluminum foil. Wrap a piece of bacon around each mushroom and secure with a toothpick. Place the mushrooms on the prepared pan. Brush each mushroom with the barbecue sauce, reserving some for a second basting. Bake for 10 minutes, baste with the remaining barbecue sauce, then return to the oven and bake for an additional 8 to 10 minutes, until the bacon is crispy. Serve warm.

# MEASURING

| 2 | | 1 | | 2 | | 3 | | 4 | | 5 | | 6 |

Many years ago, when my children were small, I discovered a storybook called *Fibblestax*. I was enchanted not only by the priceless story but also by the way the words—larger-than-life words—were lavishly and artfully printed on the page. Certain hand-painted words became the backdrop behind another layer of art, hinting at their stardom in this story of a little boy who was given the challenge of bestowing names on the unnamed objects in his village.

After reading *Fibblestax*, I couldn't contain my desire for my children to learn love and respect for words. I wanted them to see that words are important. I wanted them to appreciate the beauty and logic in how certain words sound. I wanted them to recognize how written words can be a true art form. Mostly I longed for them to know that words change lives and relationships—that they have the power to hurt and the power to heal.

After closing the book early that afternoon, I was inspired to add a little mystery and drama to our bedtime story that evening, to make this message more memorable. After baths, I lit a few candles in the dark bedroom. They giggled just a little, wondering what awaited them there, as I led them into the soft flickering light. We sat in a circle on the floor. Our faces were illuminated by the glow of candlelight as I whispered the story from beginning to end—as if it were a secret. I believe we did discover a secret that night, a secret that has served us well throughout our lives: Words change lives, they do.

To Measure:
to Select or
regulate with caution

# Rustic Vegetable Breakfast Bake

This has become my new favorite breakfast casserole because it's so easy to prepare and brimming with my favorite vegetables. Leftovers heat up quickly in the microwave (60 to 70 seconds on high power per serving).

### SERVES 10 TO 12

3 tablespoons salted butter

2 tablespoons canola oil

1 small yellow onion, chopped

8 ounces mushrooms, sliced

½ red bell pepper, seeded and coarsely chopped

1 cup chopped broccoli florets

2 cups frozen hash brown potatoes

2 cups shredded white cheddar cheese

8 large eggs, beaten

1 cup biscuit baking mix

2 cups milk

Salt and freshly ground black pepper

Preheat the oven to 400°F. Coat a 13 by 9-inch baking dish with nonstick cooking spray.

Melt the butter in a large skillet and add the canola oil. Add the onion, mushrooms, red bell pepper, broccoli, and hash browns. Sauté for about 4 minutes, or until the onion is soft. Transfer the vegetables to the baking dish. Top with 1½ cups of the cheese.

In a large mixing bowl, combine the beaten eggs, biscuit mix, milk, salt, and pepper. Beat well and pour over the vegetable mixture. Bake for 35 to 40 minutes, until a knife inserted in the center comes out clean. Top with the remaining ½ cup cheese. Let rest for 5 minutes before cutting and serving. Cover and refrigerate leftovers for up to 5 days.

# Southwestern Chicken Pasta

This is my sister Jan's recipe. We used to split this dish at a café near her home until they took it off the menu—although we can't figure out why, because it really is yummy. Thank you, Jan, for taking the time to re-create this recipe for all of us to share. You may want to substitute the tortilla chips in this recipe with the Salt and Pepper Tortilla Strips (page 143) to make it even more festive.

**SERVES 6 TO 8**

½ cup diced red bell pepper

½ cup diced red onion

1 medium tomato, diced

½ cup sliced black olives

½ cup broken tortilla chips

8 ounces farfalle pasta

3 tablespoons salted butter

1 teaspoon minced garlic

¾ cup chicken broth

3 tablespoons all-purpose flour

1 cup half-and-half

½ cup shredded Parmesan cheese

2 tablespoons salsa of your choice

Salt and freshly ground black pepper

4 grilled chicken breasts, thinly sliced

Place the prepared red bell pepper, onion, tomato, olives, and tortilla chips in separate dishes. Set aside for topping when ready to serve.

Prepare the pasta according to the package directions. Meanwhile, melt the butter in a large saucepan over medium heat. Sauté the garlic in the butter for 1 minute. Add ½ cup of the chicken broth and stir. Combine the flour and the remaining ¼ cup of the chicken broth in a small lidded container and shake until blended. Add the flour mixture to the saucepan and stir until smooth. Gradually add the half-and-half, Parmesan cheese, salsa, and salt and pepper to taste. Blend well and remove from the heat.

Drain the pasta and add to the saucepan, mixing well. To serve, layer the ingredients on a platter, beginning with the pasta mixture, then the grilled chicken, and then the toppings.

# Spinach & Feta Bake

The colors in this dish will make everyone at your table smile. This good-for-your-soul recipe is great for any time of day, and I predict it will become a new favorite!

**SERVES 6**

2 tablespoons salted butter

½ red bell pepper, chopped

½ medium yellow onion, chopped

3 cups loosely packed baby spinach

½ cup milk

8 large eggs

Salt and freshly ground black pepper

½ cup crumbled feta cheese

Preheat the oven to 350°F. Butter a 9-inch pie pan or baking dish.

In a medium skillet, melt the butter and add the bell pepper and onion. Cook over medium heat, stirring occasionally, until the vegetables are tender-crisp, 3 to 4 minutes. Add the spinach and continue cooking, stirring occasionally, until the spinach is wilted. Transfer the spinach mixture to the prepared baking dish.

In a medium bowl, whisk together the milk, eggs, salt, and pepper. Pour this mixture over the top of the spinach mixture. Top with the cheese and bake for 30 to 35 minutes, until the eggs are set in the center and the edges are lightly browned. Let stand for 5 minutes before cutting into wedges to serve.

# Parmesan Pork Tenderloin

The flavors in this dish remind me of my grandmother's cooking: faithful, old-fashioned, and deeply satisfying. The use of a slow cooker makes this recipe a great option for a busy day.

**SERVES 4 TO 6**

1 medium yellow onion, chopped

2 ribs celery, sliced into ½-inch pieces

3 carrots, peeled and sliced into ½-inch pieces

4 small potatoes, peeled and cut into 1-inch pieces

¼ cup grated Parmesan cheese

½ teaspoon dried sage

1 teaspoon seasoned salt

1 (2-pound) pork loin

1½ cups chicken broth

½ cup sherry

Place the onion, celery, carrots, and potatoes in the bottom of a 4 to 6-quart slow cooker.

Spoon the cheese, sage, and seasoned salt onto a sheet of waxed paper. Mix with your fingers. Roll the pork loin through this mixture until covered on all sides. Place the pork on top of the vegetables in the slow cooker. Then pour the chicken broth and sherry overall and cover with a lid. Cook on low for 6 hours.

Remove the pork and vegetables from the slow cooker. Arrange on a large platter and serve warm.

# chicken ham & tomato casserole

This is a beautiful and wholesome dish. Serve with steamed broccoli on the side for a perfect meal. The colors in this particular combination of foods just cheer me up!

**SERVES 4**

¼ cup all-purpose flour

½ teaspoon salt

Freshly ground black pepper

4 boneless, skinless chicken breasts

3 tablespoons vegetable oil

4 ounces cooked ham, cubed

1 (15-ounce) can diced tomatoes, drained

½ cup brown rice

¾ cup chicken broth

½ teaspoon dried basil

¼ teaspoon dried thyme

Preheat the oven to 350°F. Coat a 2½-quart baking dish with nonstick cooking spray. On a piece of waxed paper, combine the flour, salt, and pepper. Coat the chicken on both sides with this mixture.

Heat the vegetable oil in a large skillet over medium heat. Brown the chicken for about 5 minutes on each side. Transfer the chicken to a plate. Add the ham, tomatoes, rice, chicken broth, basil, and thyme to the skillet. Cook for 3 minutes. Remove from the heat and transfer to the prepared baking dish. Lay the chicken breasts on top of the rice mixture. Cover and bake until the rice is tender, about 1 hour. Serve hot.

# Black Bean & Sweet Pepper Casserole

This is a great dish with a bit of a Southwestern flair. I like serving it with grilled chicken. This recipe makes a generous amount, so one suggestion for any leftovers would be to reheat in the oven for 15 to 20 minutes, until the cheese has melted, to serve as a dip with tortilla chips.

**SERVES 10 TO 12**

1 red onion, chopped

2 cloves garlic, minced

1 red bell pepper, seeded and chopped

1 yellow bell pepper, seeded and chopped

1 tablespoon olive oil

1 (15-ounce) can diced tomatoes, with juice

1 cup of your favorite tomato salsa

1 teaspoon ground cumin

1 (15-ounce) can black beans, rinsed and drained

1 (7-ounce) can corn, drained

8 corn tortillas, cut into ½-inch strips

1 cup shredded Monterey Jack cheese

1 cup shredded pepper Jack cheese

Preheat the oven to 350°F. Coat a 13 by 9-inch baking dish with nonstick cooking spray. In a large skillet over medium heat, sauté the onion, garlic, and bell peppers in the oil, stirring, for 3 to 4 minutes. Then add the tomatoes, salsa, cumin, beans, and corn. Simmer for an additional 5 to 7 minutes, until the liquid is reduced by half.

Spread half of the bean mixture in the bottom of the baking dish. Sprinkle with half of the tortilla strips and half of the cheeses. Add the remaining half of the bean mixture, reserving the remaining cheeses for later. Coat a sheet of aluminum foil with cooking spray and cover the baking dish with it. Bake for 25 minutes.

Remove the foil and scatter the remaining strips with the reserved cheeses over the top. Return to the oven uncovered and bake for an additional 15 minutes. Let stand for at least 5 minutes before serving hot.

# Stuffed Shells

Okay, we're cheating just a little bit with this recipe. We're going to get that wonderful homemade taste and great presentation, but we're going to use a jar of store-bought spaghetti sauce to accomplish it.

**SERVES 6**

25 jumbo pasta shells

2 cups ricotta cheese

8 ounces mozzarella cheese

¾ cup grated Parmesan cheese

2 large eggs, lightly beaten

1 teaspoon salt

¼ teaspoon freshly ground black pepper

½ pound ground beef chuck

1 (28-ounce) jar tomato-based pasta sauce (I use garden-style)

Preheat the oven to 350°F. Coat a 13 by 9-inch baking dish with nonstick cooking spray.

Prepare the shells according to the package instructions.

In a large bowl, combine the ricotta cheese, mozzarella cheese, ½ cup of the Parmesan cheese, the eggs, salt, and pepper. Blend well. Fill each shell with 2 tablespoons of the cheese mixture.

In a large skillet, brown the ground chuck over medium-high heat. Add the pasta sauce to the browned meat and mix well.

Spread a thin layer of meat sauce in the bottom of the baking dish. Place the filled shells on top of the sauce. Cover the shells with the remaining sauce. Sprinkle the remaining ¼ cup of Parmesan cheese over all. Bake for 30 to 35 minutes, until bubbly.

Recipe

# Chicken with Snow Peas and Mushrooms

The first time I served this chicken dish, I enjoyed it so much that I found myself pulling my fork across my empty plate over and over, hoping to find at least one more taste left there. This will take less than an hour to prepare.

### SERVES 4

4 boneless, skinless chicken breasts

Sea salt and freshly ground black pepper

2 tablespoons vegetable oil

All-purpose flour, for dredging

1 (12-ounce) package frozen snow peas

2 tablespoons salted butter

½ cup diced yellow onion

8 ounces shiitake mushrooms, sliced

1½ cups chicken broth

1 cup heavy cream

Preheat the oven to 350°F. Season the chicken with the salt and pepper.

Add 1 tablespoon of the oil to a large skillet over medium heat. Place some flour on a plate. Dredge 2 of the chicken breasts in the flour, shaking off any excess, and place in the skillet. Cook until golden brown, about 2 minutes per side; transfer to a 13 by 9-inch baking dish. Repeat with the remaining 1 tablespoon oil and the chicken breasts. Cover the dish loosely with aluminum foil and bake for 20 to 25 minutes, until the juices run clear.

Prepare the snap peas according to the package directions. Place the skillet back on the burner over medium heat. Add the butter, then the onion and mushrooms. Stir and cook for about 4 minutes, browning the onion and mushrooms. Add the chicken broth, scraping up any browned bits with a wooden spoon. Bring to a boil and continue to cook until the liquid is reduced by half, about 3 minutes. Add the cream and cook until the sauce thickens slightly, about 4 minutes. Stir in the snap peas and heat through. Decrease the heat to low until the chicken has finished baking. Serve the vegetables over the top of the warm chicken breasts.

# BAKED ZITI

This dish is a people pleaser with children and adults alike. I usually serve it with a salad and the Soft Garlic Breadsticks (page 78). Very satisfying!

**SERVES 6 TO 8**

1 carrot, peeled and grated

1 yellow onion, diced

2 tablespoons salted butter

1 (28-ounce) can diced tomatoes, with juice

1 (15-ounce) can tomato sauce

1 (6-ounce) can tomato paste

1 clove garlic, minced

1 teaspoon sugar

2 teaspoons dried basil

2 bay leaves

Salt and freshly ground black pepper

1 pound lean ground beef

1 teaspoon dried oregano

¼ cup dry white wine

1 (1-pound) package ziti

1 (1-pound) package shredded mozzarella cheese

½ cup grated Parmesan cheese

Preheat the oven to 350°F. Coat a 13 by 9-inch baking dish with nonstick cooking spray.

In a large pot, sauté the carrot and onion in the butter over medium heat until the onion turns translucent. Add the tomatoes, tomato sauce, tomato paste, garlic, sugar, basil, bay leaves, salt, and pepper. Bring to a boil, then lower the heat, cover, and simmer for 30 minutes.

In a separate skillet over medium heat, brown the beef. Add the beef to the tomato mixture, along with the oregano and wine. Simmer for an additional 30 minutes.

Cook the ziti according to the package directions. Drain and mix with the sauce in the prepared baking dish. Top with the cheeses and bake uncovered for 25 to 30 minutes, until the cheese is bubbly.

# Fettuccine
## with Asiago and Parmesan Cheeses

This very short and simple list of ingredients combines to reward us with a rich dish. While the pasta is boiling, you can put together a nice salad to serve on the side.

**SERVES 6**

8 ounces fettuccine

1 cup grated Asiago cheese

1 cup grated Parmesan cheese

1 cup crème fraîche

A few fresh thyme leaves

Preheat the oven to 375°F. Bring a large pot of water to a boil, adding a little salt to the water. Add the fettuccine and cook according to the package directions.

Combine ¾ cup of the Asiago and ¾ cup of the Parmesan in a large bowl. Add the crème fraîche and thyme.

Remove the pasta from the water with tongs and toss with the cheese mixture. Add a little pasta water to thin, if needed.

Coat a 2-quart baking dish with nonstick cooking spray. Turn the pasta into the baking dish and sprinkle with the reserved ¼ cup of each cheese. Bake for 20 to 25 minutes, until the cheese is bubbly. Serve warm.

# Asian Orange Pork

We have seen many great food establishments come into the growing resort community where I live in the past few years. But unfortunately, we don't have many options for good Asian food. Here is an affordable and very tasty recipe that comes to my rescue when I have that particular longing.

**SERVES 4 TO 6**

3 tablespoons vegetable oil

2 pounds boneless pork shoulder, cut into bite-size pieces

Salt and seasoned pepper

¾ cup chopped scallions, white and green parts

2 cups sliced mushrooms

1 cup brown rice

1 (14-ounce) can chicken broth

½ cup freshly squeezed orange juice

3 tablespoons soy sauce

¼ teaspoon ground ginger

2 teaspoons grated orange zest

1 cup frozen peas, thawed

Preheat the oven to 350°F. Lightly coat a 2½-quart casserole dish with cooking spray.

In a large skillet, warm 2 tablespoons of the oil over medium-high heat. Season the pork with salt and seasoned pepper and add to the skillet. Brown the pork, stirring occasionally, for about 8 minutes. Transfer the browned pork to the casserole dish.

In the same skillet, over medium heat, heat the remaining 1 tablespoon vegetable oil. Sauté the scallions and mushrooms until tender, about 5 minutes. Stir in the rice, broth, orange juice, soy sauce, ginger, and orange zest. Bring to a boil and then pour over the pork in the casserole dish.

Cover and bake until the rice is tender and most of the liquid is absorbed, about 45 minutes. Stir in the peas and cook, uncovered, for 10 minutes longer. Serve hot.

# Filled Sole Roll-Ups

I like the interesting presentation of this fish dish. The rolled fish bundles, with the bright spinach inside, seem almost like a present. It's a nice reminder for me that food really is a gift.

### SERVES 4

8 tablespoons butter, melted

2 tablespoons freshly squeezed lemon juice

6 to 8 sole fillets, about 4 ounces each

Salt and freshly ground black pepper

1 cup loosely packed spinach

1 cup cooked brown rice

½ cup grated Swiss cheese

Paprika, for sprinkling

Preheat the oven to 400°F. Coat an 8-inch square baking dish with nonstick cooking spray. Mix the butter and lemon juice in a cup.

Lay the fillets on a sheet of waxed paper. Season with salt and pepper. Place a few leaves of spinach on top of each fillet. Evenly distribute the rice over the top of the spinach. Then do the same with the cheese. Drizzle about a tablespoon of the butter and lemon mixture over each fillet. Roll each up and secure with toothpicks. Place each bundle in the prepared baking dish. Drizzle the remaining butter mixture over the top of each bundle. Sprinkle with paprika.

Bake uncovered until bubbly and the fish flakes, about 15 minutes. Serve hot.

# Chicken Tortilla Soup

Don't let the long list of ingredients intimidate you! This recipe is well worth the time and effort. If you have a Saturday morning to play in the kitchen, you'll enjoy the aroma that fills your home as the soup simmers. After you have completed the recipe, you will have a bonus: an extra quart or so of chicken stock that you can store in the freezer for a future dish. To make the garnish for this soup a little more special, try serving it with the Salt and Pepper Tortilla Strips (page 143) rather than just plain chips.

### SERVES 8 TO 10

1 (3-pound) chicken

2 ribs celery, cut into chunks

1 carrot, peeled and quartered

1 medium yellow onion, quartered

2 tablespoons chicken soup base

2 teaspoons seasoned salt

1 clove garlic, minced

1 teaspoon freshly ground black pepper

4 to 6 medium potatoes, peeled and chopped

1 (15-ounce) can creamed corn

1 (10-ounce) can Rotel tomatoes with chiles, crushed

1½ cups half-and-half

3 tablespoons minced fresh cilantro

2 cups shredded Monterey Jack–cheddar cheese blend

1 (9-ounce) bag tortilla chips

Combine the chicken, celery, carrot, onion, chicken soup base, seasoned salt, garlic, and pepper in a large stockpot. Cover with water by about 2 inches. Bring to a boil and then lower the heat to a simmer. Cook for about 1 hour, or until the chicken is tender and falling off the bone. Remove the chicken from the bones and cut into small pieces. Strain and reserve the broth.

Wipe out the stockpot, and boil the potatoes in about 4 cups of the reserved broth in the pot. When the potatoes are tender, remove from the heat. Leaving the potatoes in the broth, carefully blend with an immersion blender until smooth. If you don't have an immersion blender, you can mash the potatoes with a fork. Add the corn, tomatoes, and half-and-half. Simmer this mixture over low heat for 15 to 20 minutes. Add some remaining reserved chicken broth if the mixture seems too thick. Taste and adjust the seasoning if needed, and add the cooked chicken to the soup.

When ready to serve, pass the cilantro, cheese, and tortilla chips at the table for topping the soup.

# Parmesan Tilapia with Roasted Vegetables

This is a "new and improved" version of a recipe I used to prepare for our family. I'll always remember it as the first "recipe call" I received from my adult son, Blake. He was in his last year of college and called to ask me to talk him through it so that he could prepare it for his roommates. Moms everywhere know—this is one of those memories you file away as extra special. These big boys don't know it, but to us it's as if they are saying, "You know that amazing dish you make? I've always loved it almost as much as I love you, and I'd like to share it with my friends." Of course, this isn't what they say. They just say, "How do I make that fish thing?" And we share the recipe. But when we hang up the phone, we can't quit smiling for five minutes.

Olive oil

Grated Parmesan cheese (about 1 tablespoon per fillet)

Fresh or frozen tilapia fillets, about
4 ounces each (1 to 2 per guest)

A variety of chopped vegetables (some good
choices: red potatoes, onions, sweet red or yellow
peppers, mushrooms, carrots, broccoli)

Garlic salt

Freshly ground black pepper

Crushed butter-flavored crackers
(about 1 cracker for every 2 fillets)

Freshly squeezed lemon juice (about 1 lemon per 4 servings)

Your favorite prepared rice (1 cup per person)

Preheat the oven to 425°F. Line a large baking sheet with parchment paper and brush olive oil on the paper.

Sprinkle the Parmesan cheese over the parchment paper. Brush the fish fillets with olive oil on both sides and lay on top of the cheese, using one half of the space on the parchment paper, reserving the other half for the vegetables.

Arrange the vegetables on the other half of the parchment paper and drizzle with olive oil. Scatter the Parmesan cheese over the fish and vegetables. Season the fish and vegetables with garlic salt and pepper. Sprinkle the crushed crackers over the fish. Bake for 20 to 22 minutes, until the fish is flaky when pricked with a fork. Drizzle each fillet with lemon juice. Serve with rice.

# Creamy Tomato Basil Soup

Be sure to look at the recipe for Asiago Croutons when planning the preparation of this soup. You'll enjoy the flavor of this soup so much that you'll find it difficult to believe it's also so healthy.

## SERVES 12

¼ cup olive oil

2 tablespoons salted butter

2 large yellow onions, finely chopped

1 clove garlic, minced

¼ cup all-purpose flour

1 (32-ounce) container chicken broth

2 (28-ounce) cans crushed tomatoes

1 tablespoon sugar

Salt and freshly ground black pepper

2 cups half-and-half

⅓ cup chopped fresh basil

4 cups Asiago Croutons (page 92)

In a 4-quart stockpot, heat the oil and butter over medium heat until the butter melts. Add the onions and sauté for about 6 minutes, or until the onions are soft but not browned. Add the garlic and sauté for an additional minute. Add the flour and stir for another minute. Slowly add the chicken broth, stirring until well combined. Add the tomatoes, sugar, salt, and pepper. Decrease the heat to low and let simmer for about 45 minutes.

Using an immersion blender, carefully puree the soup for 30 to 60 seconds, being careful not to splatter the hot liquid. If you don't have an immersion blender, you may transfer the soup in small batches to a blender to puree. Then return it to the large stockpot.

Warm the half-and-half in the microwave for 45 seconds on high power. Right before serving, add the half-and-half to the soup and stir to combine. Top each serving with a sprinkling of basil and croutons.

# CHUNKY CHICKEN SALAD SANDWICHES

I served a slightly sweet chicken salad for years at my first restaurant and it always got rave reviews (see the recipe for Chicken Salad for 100 of Your Closest Friends, page 49). But in the past year, I've worked hard to create lighter versions of many of my favorite foods. This is the chicken salad I enjoy the most now, knowing that I can eat it without guilt. It's great on thick slices of whole wheat bread. But you can also eat it on a bed of baby romaine, with a few crisp crackers on the side.

**SERVES 6**

3 cups chopped cooked chicken

½ cup diced cucumber

½ cup minced celery

¼ cup chopped fresh chives

½ cup light mayonnaise

¼ cup freshly squeezed lemon juice

Salt and freshly ground black pepper

1 (8-ounce) package baby romaine lettuce

12 slices whole-grain bread

Combine the chicken, cucumber, celery, chives, mayonnaise, lemon juice, salt, and pepper in a medium bowl. Adjust the seasoning to taste.

To assemble the sandwiches, layer the romaine and then the chicken mixture between 2 slices of bread. Cut the sandwiches on the diagonal and serve.

# Shepherd's Pie

This is one of my favorite "snow day" recipes. Of course, it tastes great any time of year and in climates with or without snow! But it definitely falls into my comfort food category.

### SERVES 4 TO 6

2 pounds russet potatoes, peeled and cubed

½ cup milk or cream, warmed slightly

10 tablespoons butter, at room temperature

2 tablespoons sour cream (optional)

Salt and freshly ground black pepper

1½ pounds ground beef, lamb, or turkey

1 carrot, peeled and finely chopped

1 medium yellow onion, finely chopped

1 rib celery, chopped

2 cloves garlic, minced

1 tablespoon all-purpose flour

1½ cups beef broth

1 tablespoon Worcestershire sauce

½ cup frozen peas

In a large saucepan, boil the potatoes in water to cover over medium-high heat until fork-tender, about 20 minutes. Drain the potatoes and transfer to a mixing bowl. Add the milk, 8 tablespoons of the butter, and the sour cream, if using. Beat together until smooth and season with salt and pepper to taste. Set aside.

Preheat the oven to 350°F. Brown the ground beef in a large skillet over medium heat. If you are using ground lamb or turkey rather than beef, you may want to coat the pan with nonstick cooking spray first. Drain the fat off the meat and transfer the meat to a bowl.

In the same pan, melt the remaining 2 tablespoons butter. Add the carrot, onion, celery, and garlic. Sauté over medium heat until the onion is soft, about 5 minutes. Add the flour and mix well. Add the beef broth and cook, stirring, for about 1 minute. Add the Worcestershire, cooked meat, and frozen peas. Stir to combine, mixing well. Remove from the heat.

Transfer the meat mixture to a deep-dish pie plate or casserole dish. Season with salt and pepper. Add the mashed potatoes on top, spreading to the edge of the dish. Bake until golden, 12 to 15 minutes. Serve hot.

# The Best Beef Stew

Because this stew requires 2 to 3 hours to prepare from start to finish,
I like making this recipe the night before serving it. Then it's just a quick ten
minutes of preparation time before dinner. The flavor is rich and no one ever
leaves the table hungry. I usually serve it with corn muffins or biscuits.

### SERVES 10 TO 12

3 pounds beef chuck roast, trimmed and cut into 1½-inch cubes

Salt and freshly ground black pepper

¼ cup vegetable oil

1 medium yellow onion, chopped

3 cloves garlic, minced

3 tablespoons all-purpose flour

1 cup dry red wine

1 (14.5-ounce) can chicken broth

1 bay leaf

1 teaspoon dried thyme

6 medium russet potatoes, peeled and cut into 1-inch cubes

5 carrots, peeled and sliced

1 cup frozen peas, thawed

Preheat the oven to 300°F. Dry the beef with paper towels and season the beef with salt and pepper. In a large skillet, heat 1 tablespoon of the vegetable oil over medium-high heat. Add one-third of the beef to the skillet and cook until well browned, 2 to 3 minutes. Using tongs, turn each piece and continue cooking until all sides are well browned. Transfer these pieces of meat to a Dutch oven. Brown the remaining beef in the same manner in two separate batches, adding 1 tablespoon of the vegetable oil before browning each batch.

Lower the heat to medium and add the remaining 1 table-spoon oil to the skillet. Add the onion and ½ teaspoon salt. Cook, stirring frequently, scraping the pot bottom with a wooden spoon to loosen the browned bits, until the onion has softened, about 4 minutes. Add the garlic and continue to cook for another 30 seconds. Add the flour. Cook and stir for about 1 minute longer.

Gradually add the wine, scraping and stirring until the liquid is smooth and thick, about 2 minutes. Gradually add the chicken broth, stirring until well blended. Add the bay leaf and thyme. Simmer for 1 minute. Pour this mixture over the browned beef in the Dutch oven. Cover with a lid and bake for 1 hour.

Remove the Dutch oven from the oven and add the potatoes and carrots. Cover and return to the oven for 1 more hour.

Remove from the oven and add the peas. Cover and let stand for 5 minutes. Serve hot.

# mike's mexican chicken soup

I have known Mike Tuley since he was a middle school student and I was a physical education teacher. I'm happy that our paths have crossed again, this time in the kitchen rather than in the gym. He is an excellent cook, and I consider him to be an expert in the area of Mexican food. So I asked him to create this soup for the Paint Box Café. The flavors are so rich and deep, and it is incredibly good for you. By leaving out the chicken and the cheese, you will be able to serve this beautiful soup to your vegan friends as well.

**SERVES 10 TO 12**

1 poblano chile pepper

1 red bell pepper

1 green bell pepper

Canola oil

Salt and freshly ground black pepper

2 tablespoons olive oil

1 medium yellow onion, chopped

2 cloves garlic, minced

3 tablespoons ground cumin

1 tablespoon crushed dried Mexican oregano

1 tablespoon ground ancho chile pepper

1 (28-ounce) can crushed tomatoes

1 (4-ounce) can diced green chiles, chopped

4 (14.5-ounce) cans vegetable broth

2 cups cooked diced chicken

Juice of 3 limes

3 cups rice

1 (14.5-ounce) can black beans, rinsed and drained

1 (8-ounce) package shredded Monterey Jack–cheddar cheese blend

Tortilla strips, for garnish

Preheat the oven to 375°F. Place the poblano chile, red bell pepper, and green bell pepper on a baking sheet. Drizzle with canola oil and season with salt and pepper. Roast for 15 minutes. Remove from the oven, place the peppers in a resealable plastic bag, and seal. Set aside and let the peppers rest for 15 minutes.

Meanwhile, place the olive oil in a stockpot over medium heat. Sauté the onion and garlic in the olive oil until the onion is soft but not brown.

Take the peppers out of the bag and remove the skin. Cut the peppers open, remove and discard the seeds, and dice each pepper into ⅜-inch pieces. Add the diced peppers to the onion mixture. Add the cumin, Mexican oregano, ground chile pepper, crushed tomatoes, green chiles, and vegetable broth. Mix well and continue to cook over medium heat until the soup comes to a boil. Decrease the heat to low and simmer for 30 minutes.

Remove the soup from the heat and let cool slightly. Transfer half of the soup to a food processor and blend for 30 seconds. Return the blended soup to the stockpot and add the diced chicken and lime juice.

Prepare the rice according to the package directions. Place the rice and the beans in separate bowls. When ready to serve, ladle one serving of rice, 2 tablespoons beans, and a generous amount of soup into each bowl. Top with the shredded cheese and tortilla strips.

# Italian Garden Pasta Soup

Such a rich and hearty soup, and so full of flavor! Every bite is loaded with vegetables. Consider serving it with the Soft Garlic Breadsticks (page 78). Perfection.

**SERVES 8**

1 pound lean ground beef

1 cup diced yellow onions

1 cup julienned carrots

1 cup diced celery

2 cloves garlic, minced

1 (28-ounce) can diced tomatoes, with juice

1 (15-ounce) can dark red kidney beans, rinsed and drained

1 (24-ounce) can great northern beans, rinsed and drained

1 (15-ounce) can tomato sauce

1 (12-ounce) can tomato or tomato-vegetable juice

1 teaspoon white vinegar

1 teaspoon salt

1 teaspoon dried oregano

1 teaspoon dried basil

½ teaspoon dried thyme

½ teaspoon freshly ground black pepper

4 ounces miniature farfalle pasta

8 ounces Parmesan cheese, shaved

Brown the beef in a large stockpot over medium heat. Drain off the fat. Add the onions, carrots, celery, and garlic and sauté for 10 minutes. Add the diced tomatoes, kidney beans, great northern beans, tomato sauce, tomato juice, vinegar, salt, oregano, basil, thyme, and pepper. Simmer for about 1 hour.

Meanwhile, prepare the pasta according to the package directions, undercooking it by a minute or two. Drain well and add to the soup. Simmer for about 10 minutes. When ready to serve, top with the Parmesan cheese.

# Rosemary Pork with Roasted Vegetables

I like serving this dish with brown rice and warm bread. You'll see the use of seasoned pepper in this recipe. I learned about this pepper from my friends, Judy and Barb. Now I use it regularly in most of my recipes.

**SERVES 8**

½ cup olive oil

1 pound baby carrots

2 medium yellow onions, quartered

3 teaspoons salt

2 teaspoons seasoned pepper

3 tablespoons fresh rosemary leaves

1 (4-pound) boneless pork loin roast

2 tablespoons Dijon mustard

2 cloves garlic, minced

¼ cup balsamic vinegar

Preheat the oven to 425°F. Place 3 tablespoons of the olive oil in a large skillet over medium-high heat. Add the carrots and onions to the hot oil and season with about half of the salt and half of the pepper. Sauté the vegetables for about 8 minutes, or until caramelized. Remove from the heat and stir in about half of the rosemary.

Transfer the vegetables to a large roasting pan. Place the pork on top of the vegetables. Season the pork with the remaining half of the salt and pepper. Combine the mustard, garlic, the remaining 5 tablespoons olive oil, and the remaining half of the rosemary. Spread this mixture over the top of the pork. Bake for about 1 hour and 10 minutes, or until a meat thermometer inserted into the thickest portion of the pork registers 160°F. Let stand for 10 minutes.

Transfer the pork to a serving platter. Surround the pork with the vegetables. Add the vinegar to the reserved drippings in the pan and bring to a boil. Decrease the heat to medium and simmer, stirring often, until reduced by about one-quarter. Pour the sauce over the vegetables and serve.

# Jack's Gumbo

I'm so happy I had the chance to meet and become friends with Jack and Linda Hostetter. For the past few years, when the subject of Jack's famous gumbo would come up in conversations with friends, everyone would cry in unison, "You need to get Jack's gumbo recipe for your next book!" He was gracious enough to share it with me. Jack says the secret is in the roux, which is the stage of the recipe where flour is added for thickening.

**SERVES 6 TO 8**

14 ounces andouille sausage, sliced into 1-inch pieces

3 boneless, skinless chicken breasts, cut into 1-inch pieces

¾ cup vegetable oil

¾ cup all-purpose flour

2 cups finely chopped yellow onions

¾ cup chopped green bell pepper

¾ cup sliced celery

2 tablespoons minced fresh flat-leaf parsley

3 (15-ounce) cans chicken broth

1½ teaspoons dried thyme

10 whole allspice berries, or ½ teaspoon ground allspice

½ teaspoon ground mace

8 whole cloves, or ½ teaspoon ground cloves

¼ teaspoon cayenne pepper

3 bay leaves

3 teaspoons salt

1 teaspoon freshly ground black pepper

1 cup frozen okra and/or 1 cup frozen corn (optional)

8 cups cooked rice of your choice, for serving

In a large skillet over medium heat, brown the sausage. Remove the sausage and set aside. In the same skillet, cook the chicken in the sausage drippings until done; remove and set aside with the sausage.

In the same skillet, over medium-low to medium heat, warm the oil. Add the flour, stirring continuously until the roux becomes medium brown in color. Be patient—this could take up to 20 minutes, and you don't want to scorch the roux or it will be unusable.

Stir in the onions, bell pepper, celery, and parsley and cook for 10 minutes over medium-low heat. Again, be careful not to scorch. Add the chicken broth, sausage, and chicken. Then stir in the thyme, allspice, mace, cloves, cayenne, bay leaves, salt, and pepper. Bring to a boil and then decrease the heat and let simmer for about 1 hour.

Add the okra and/or corn, if using, and heat through. Serve over the rice.

# LEIGH ANN'S EASY POTATO SOUP

One of my Iowa friends, Leigh Ann Whipple, sent this recipe to me the day before a big snowstorm hit the Midwest. Perfect timing, since there aren't many foods that taste better on a cold winter day than potato soup! I like Leigh Ann's recipe because there are no heavy cream-of-something canned soups as a base—just honest, fresh ingredients.

### SERVES 8

6 tablespoons salted butter

3 scallions, thinly sliced (reserve the green parts for garnish)

8 medium russet potatoes, peeled and cut into 1-inch pieces

6 cups chicken broth

¾ cup heavy cream or half-and-half

Salt and freshly ground black pepper

2 cups shredded cheddar cheese

10 slices bacon, cooked and crumbled

In a large stockpot, melt 3 tablespoons of the butter over medium heat and sauté the white parts of the scallions until soft, about 2 minutes. Add the potatoes and chicken broth to the pot and cook for about 30 minutes, or until the potatoes are fork-tender.

Decrease the heat to low. Using an immersion blender or a large fork, mash the potatoes in the pot, being careful not to splash the hot liquid. Add the remaining 3 tablespoons of butter, the cream, and salt and pepper to taste.

Serve hot with the cheese, bacon, and sliced scallion greens on the side for topping the soup.

# Chicken Salad For 100 of Your Closest Friends

One day I found myself preparing food for about 100 people who would be attending a fund-raiser for a friend of mine who was running for office. It occurred to me that I might not be the only one who would appreciate having a large-quantity recipe at my fingertips. It seems that large crowd functions are, more often than not, planned with a budget in mind. So I'm hoping that having this recipe on hand will help in that regard.

You may serve about ½ cup of this chicken salad on a bed of lettuce, or use the same amount to make a sandwich. Allow 3 to 4 hours for preparation. To save time, you may purchase the roasted chickens in the deli section of most grocery stores.

### SERVES ABOUT 100

10 roasted chickens

1 (32-ounce) jar light mayonnaise

1 (24-ounce) jar sweet pickle relish

1 bunch celery, trimmed and diced

1 pound white seedless grapes, halved

12 large eggs, hard-cooked, peeled, and chopped

1 tablespoon sugar

Salt

Remove the skin and bones from the roasted chickens. I wear rubber gloves to do this, since it takes about an hour to work through this many chickens. Then, using kitchen shears, cut the chicken into small pieces. Transfer the chicken into a large bowl (one large enough to hold at least 15 quarts). If you don't have a bowl this large, you may mix it in smaller batches.

Add the jars of mayonnaise and relish. Follow with the celery, grapes, and eggs. Sprinkle the sugar over all. Mix well to combine. Add salt to taste. Cover and chill. The chicken salad will keep in the refrigerator for up to 3 days.

**49**

# Bella Burgers

There is a large piece of art hanging in my daughter's bedroom announcing: "You are beauty full." I wanted this to be the message she woke up to each morning. So it's fitting that this vegetarian recipe created by Brooke would be titled bella, which is Italian for "beautiful." The thing that impressed me the most about this hearty sandwich was how satisfying it was without being heavy. I've included all the extras Brooke adds to make it into the masterpiece she and her "beauty-full" friends enjoy so much.

### SERVES 4

3 tablespoons olive oil

4 large portobello mushrooms, stemmed

1 small zucchini, sliced into ¼-inch pieces

1 small yellow onion, chopped

1 red bell pepper, seeded and chopped

Salt and freshly ground black pepper

Vegetable seasoning (you will find some choices
in the spice aisle of your grocery store)

4 whole-grain sandwich buns, split

4 ounces feta cheese

Sun-dried tomatoes

Pesto

Hummus

Sliced avocado

Sliced tomato

Preheat the oven to 425°F. Brush a baking sheet with 1 tablespoon of the olive oil. Place the mushrooms, rounded side up, on one half of the baking sheet. On the other side, distribute the zucchini, onion, and red bell pepper. Brush all the vegetables with the remaining 2 tablespoons olive oil. Season with the salt, pepper, and vegetable seasoning. Roast for 15 to 18 minutes, until the vegetables are just tender.

Meanwhile, lay the sandwich buns open on a separate baking sheet. Scatter the feta cheese evenly over the bottom half of the buns. After removing the roasted vegetables from the oven, toast the sandwich buns with the feta for 3 to 5 minutes, just until the buns are lightly browned and the cheese has softened. Remove the buns from the oven and assemble the sandwiches. Use 1 mushroom per bun, topping each with the roasted vegetables and any of the extras, if using. Serve warm.

# Chipotle Barbecue Chicken Club Sandwiches

At the end of a long Saturday at work, I was relieved to have this recipe in my repertoire to share with some friends who were coming to dinner that night. Nearly everything can be prepared the day before so that 30 minutes is all you'll need to assemble and toast these juicy, spicy sandwiches. I served a salad on the side, but an assortment of raw vegetables and dip would also be a nice addition to round out this meal.

### SERVES 4

4 whole wheat sandwich buns, split

4 boneless, skinless chicken breasts, cooked

½ cup purchased chipotle barbecue sauce

½ cup shredded Colby–Monterey Jack cheese blend

8 slices Peppered Pecan Bacon (page 60)

Preheat the oven to 400°F. Line a baking sheet with aluminum foil and spread out the split buns on it. Place a chicken breast on the bottom of each sandwich bun. Spoon a generous amount of the barbecue sauce over each breast. Distribute the cheese evenly over the top of the sauce. Place 2 pieces of bacon on top of the sauce. Toast in the oven for 5 to 6 minutes, until the top buns are lightly toasted and the cheese is melted. Serve warm.

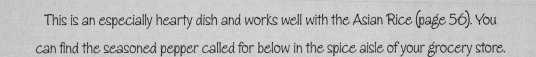

# Sweet & Sour Pork Chops

This is an especially hearty dish and works well with the Asian Rice (page 56). You can find the seasoned pepper called for below in the spice aisle of your grocery store.

### SERVES 4

2 tablespoons vegetable oil

4 boneless pork chops, 1 inch thick

Salt and seasoned pepper

1 (8-ounce) can pineapple tidbits, with juice

1 small green bell pepper, seeded and cut into 1-inch pieces

1 small red bell pepper, seeded and cut into 1-inch pieces

⅓ cup firmly packed light brown sugar

¼ cup white or rice wine vinegar

1 teaspoon soy sauce

¼ teaspoon salt

1 clove garlic, minced

2 tablespoons cornstarch

¼ cup water

Preheat the oven to 350°F. Lightly coat a 2½-quart casserole dish with nonstick cooking spray. In a medium skillet, heat the oil over medium-high heat. Add the pork chops and brown, about 5 minutes on each side. Season with salt and seasoned pepper to taste.

Transfer the chops to the casserole dish. Drain the pineapple (reserving the liquid). Distribute the pineapple, green bell pepper, and red bell pepper over the top of the pork chops.

In a small bowl, mix the brown sugar, reserved pineapple juice, vinegar, soy sauce, salt, and garlic. Pour over the chops. Cover and bake for about 50 minutes.

In another small bowl, mix the cornstarch and water. Stir into the casserole juices. Return to the oven and bake, uncovered, for an additional 8 to 10 minutes, until the juices are thickened. Serve hot.

# THE TIES THAT BIND

My daughter, Brooke, filled the pages of a journal we send back and forth across the miles with some of the details of her trip to Haiti during the summer after the 2010 earthquake. In spite of the devastation, Brooke wrote of the remarkable attitudes and, believe it or not, the joy that she witnessed among the Haitians.

She played soccer in the hot, dusty streets with the children, painted happy designs on the cinder block walls of the orphanage where they lived, and then when that project was done, let the children paint on her. She was smitten with them and hated to leave them behind at the end of her trip.

I read in another account of the earthquake about a young woman who was the same age as Brooke. This young lady lost twenty family members in the quake. She was quoted as saying, "Everyone lost something and because of that we became one." Sticks in a bundle, not easily broken, as the proverb says, and thick with their experience. And now, Brooke is part of their bundle.

TO BIND:

to stir any of a variety of ingredients

into a hot liquid, causing it to thicken

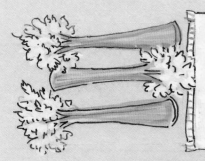

# Asian Rice

The addition of the vegetables to this basic rice dish makes it hearty, healthy, and beautiful! You can also use this as a base to create a main dish in a hurry, adding leftover chicken or pork from previous meals.

**SERVES 6**

2 teaspoons vegetable oil

½ cup chopped yellow onion

½ cup chopped red bell pepper

½ cup chopped celery

1 cup brown rice

1 (14-ounce) can chicken broth

3 tablespoons soy sauce

Salt and freshly ground black pepper

2 cups frozen stir-fry vegetables with sugar snap peas

⅓ cup sliced or slivered almonds

Preheat the oven to 350°F. Lightly coat a 2½-quart casserole with nonstick cooking spray. Heat the vegetable oil in a medium saucepan over medium heat. Sauté the onion, red bell pepper, and celery until tender, about 5 minutes. Stir in the rice, broth, soy sauce, salt, and pepper. Bring to a boil.

Transfer the mixture to the prepared casserole dish. Cover and bake for 40 minutes.

Stir in the frozen vegetables and almonds. Cover and return to the oven for an additional 10 to 15 minutes, until the rice is tender and the liquid is absorbed. Serve hot.

# Roasted Mushrooms

One of my favorite ways to serve these mushrooms is alongside a juicy sirloin steak. But they are so versatile. They are also very nice with chicken, pork, or fish. Leftovers may be tossed into a pasta salad or omelet.

### SERVES 4

2 pounds mushrooms of your choice
(a variety is nice), cut into chunks

2 tablespoons butter, melted

2 tablespoons olive oil

1 clove garlic, minced

Salt and freshly ground black pepper

Preheat the oven to 425°F. Place the mushrooms in a large zip-top plastic bag. Pour the melted butter and olive oil into the bag. Add the garlic and season with salt and pepper to taste. Close the bag and shake to coat the mushrooms evenly. Empty the contents of the bag onto a large baking sheet. Roast for 10 minutes. Remove from the oven and toss. Return to the oven and roast for an additional 5 minutes. Serve warm.

# Fake Baked Beans

This very simple recipe gives you the fun flavor of baked beans, but in half the time. Think of it each time you get ready to grill or plan a picnic.

### SERVES 4 TO 6

4 slices bacon

½ cup diced yellow onion

½ cup salsa of your choice

2 tablespoons ketchup

2 tablespoons firmly packed light or dark brown sugar

½ teaspoon ground cumin

2 (16-ounce) cans pork and beans

In a heavy skillet, cook the bacon over medium-high heat until crisp. Drain, reserving 2 tablespoons of the drippings in the pan. Crumble the bacon. Sauté the onion in the reserved drippings until tender, 2 to 3 minutes. Stir in the crumbled bacon, salsa, ketchup, brown sugar, and cumin. Add the pork and beans and bring to a boil. Lower the heat and simmer uncovered until thickened, about 15 minutes. Serve warm.

# Spiced Apples

I think it's easy to forget that fruits as well as vegetables can make a nice side dish. Apples are an excellent example. This recipe is a perfect choice served warm as a side with pork chops. It also makes a beautiful topping for ice cream or cheesecake. I use it for filling my Apple Turnovers (page 116), too.

**SERVES 6**

5 Granny Smith apples

1 teaspoon ground cinnamon

½ teaspoon ground ginger

½ teaspoon ground nutmeg

Juice of 1 lemon

1 cup water

½ cup sugar

Peel and core the apples and cut into ½-inch chunks. Toss the apples in a large bowl with the cinnamon, ginger, nutmeg, and lemon juice.

Bring the water and sugar to a boil in a large saucepan. Add the apple mixture to the sugar mixture and simmer over medium-low heat until thickened, 10 to 12 minutes. Serve warm or at room temperature.

# Peppered Pecan Bacon

I realize that this is not a typical side dish. But I just adore this bacon and felt that you would, too, so I had to include it. My favorite way to serve it, besides in the obvious breakfast venue, is on a sandwich (like the Chipotle Barbecue Chicken Club Sandwiches, page 52) or crumbled as a garnish on a salad.

### SERVES 6

¼ cup pecans, chopped

¼ cup firmly packed light brown sugar

1 tablespoon seasoned pepper

12 slices thick-cut bacon, cut in half crosswise

Preheat the oven to 400°F. Line two baking sheets with aluminum foil. Spray two wire cooling racks with nonstick cooking spray and place on the foil-lined baking sheets.

In a small bowl, combine the pecans, brown sugar, and seasoned pepper. Mix well.

Place the bacon pieces in a single layer on the prepared wire racks, about ¼ inch apart. Press the pecan mixture on top of the bacon slices, coating them well. Bake for 18 to 20 minutes, until browned and crisp. Let stand for 5 minutes before serving.

# Canopy Salad

This salad or a very similar version of it is served almost every Sunday afternoon at our little church called Canopy. Dozens of people walk in the building in the morning before the service carrying slow cookers full of soup, baskets brimming with bread, trays of tempting desserts, and bowls of sumptuous salad. It's a very informal gathering—in fact, the dining area is actually a primitive basketball court lined with folding tables and chairs. But we're a family, a sprawling, quirky collection of people of all ages. If you're in Lake of the Ozarks on a Sunday, stop in and pull up a chair. There's always room for one more.

## SERVES 8 TO 10

1 (1-pound) bag mixed greens, such as spring mix

1 cup dried cranberries

½ cup pine nuts

1 apple or pear, peeled, cored, and diced

1 cup crumbled feta cheese or 1 cup shaved Parmesan cheese

Creamy Balsamic Dressing of your choice

Combine the mixed greens, cranberries, pine nuts, fruit, and cheese in a large chilled bowl. Add the dressing at the last minute and toss before serving.

# SPinaCH SaLaD

This is a so-simple salad that pairs beautifully with a panini sandwich or slice of quiche. The farfalle pasta makes such a fun presentation. Think of this recipe the next time you're pulling a party menu together. The dressing can also be used to create a wilted spinach topping for the Spinach Baked Potatoes (page 63).

SERVES 4

**GARLIC VINAIGRETTE**

3 tablespoons extra-virgin olive oil

2 tablespoons white wine vinegar

1 teaspoon Dijon mustard

½ teaspoon seasoned pepper

½ teaspoon salt

4 cloves garlic, minced

**SALAD**

½ cup miniature farfalle pasta, prepared according to the package directions

5 to 6 cups loosely packed baby spinach

¼ cup chopped red onion

Chill 4 salad plates.

To make the vinaigrette, in a large bowl, combine the olive oil, vinegar, mustard, seasoned pepper, salt, and garlic and whisk until well blended.

Add the farfalle and toss until coated. Remove the farfalle from the bowl. Add the spinach and red onion to the dressing and toss to coat. Divide the salad evenly among the salad plates. Top with the farfalle and serve.

# SPINACH BAKED POTATOES

This recipe is a refreshing alternative to traditional baked potatoes. Both the potatoes and the spinach topping can be prepared up to a week in advance, then assembled and rewarmed in the microwave before serving.

### SERVES 4

4 Yukon gold potatoes

Olive oil

Sea salt

Garlic Vinaigrette (page 62)

¼ cup chopped red onion

4 cups loosely packed baby spinach

¼ cup crumbled feta cheese

Preheat the oven to 425°F. Scrub the potatoes and prick lightly with a fork. Lightly coat the potatoes with olive oil and sprinkle sea salt over the surface of the potatoes. Place in a baking dish. Bake uncovered for about 1 hour, until fork-tender.

Heat the vinaigrette in a large skillet over medium-high heat. Add the onion and cook for 2 minutes, stirring occasionally. Add the spinach and toss until wilted. Remove from the heat.

Split the baked potatoes open. Divide the wilted spinach among the potatoes. Top with the feta cheese and serve.

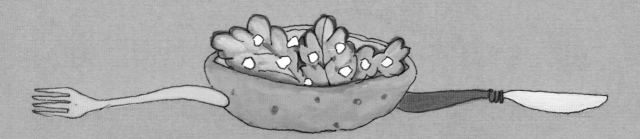

# Onion Parmesan Roasted Potatoes

This dish is perfect for a large group, since almost everyone loves potatoes. The ingredients are easy to pull together and also very affordable. The flavor reminds me of my mom's roast beef and vegetables. Since I prefer crispy potatoes, I like making this recipe a day or two in advance, and then reheating the potatoes (uncovered at 375°F) 15 or 20 minutes before serving time.

**SERVES 10 TO 12**

5 pounds red potatoes, sliced ¼ inch thick

⅔ cup vegetable oil

2 (1.25-ounce) envelopes dried onion soup mix

8 ounces Parmesan cheese, shredded

Salt and freshly ground black pepper

Preheat the oven to 350°F. Place the potatoes, oil, soup mix, cheese, and salt and pepper in a large baking pan. (I use a half sheet pan that measures 17 by 12 inches, but you can also divide the ingredients evenly between two 13 by 9-inch baking pans.) Toss the ingredients to mix and cover with aluminum foil. Bake for 40 minutes.

Remove from the oven and increase the temperature to 375°F. Remove the foil, stir carefully, and return to the oven for an additional 20 to 30 minutes. Serve hot.

# Tuscan Beans

I know it may be difficult to imagine beans as a pretty side dish. But these beans are just that! The diced tomatoes add a little splash of color, and color is a mood lifter. It's a nice choice alongside pork chops or chicken tacos, as well as burgers.

SERVES 4

½ cup diced pancetta, or 4 slices bacon, coarsely chopped

Olive oil cooking spray

½ cup chopped yellow onion

1 clove garlic, minced

2 (15-ounce) cans cannellini or great northern beans, rinsed and drained

1 (15-ounce) can diced tomatoes with juices

Salt and freshly ground black pepper

2 teaspoons balsamic vinegar

2 tablespoons chopped fresh flat-leaf parsley, for garnish

½ cup grated Parmesan cheese, for garnish

Preheat the oven to 350°F. In a small skillet, cook the pancetta over medium heat. If the pancetta seems too dry, spray with olive oil cooking spray. Add the onion and garlic and sauté until the vegetables are tender and the pancetta is crisp.

Lightly coat a 2½-quart casserole dish with olive oil cooking spray, then add the beans, tomatoes, salt and pepper, and the pancetta mixture. Mix well.

Bake uncovered until bubbly, about 35 minutes. Stir in the vinegar and garnish with the parsley and Parmesan before serving.

# Streusel-Topped Sweet Potatoes

These sweet potatoes are a really fun alternative to the casseroles and soufflés we've all had before. They just seem more personalized, somehow. We enjoyed them for the first time one recent Christmas at the Bakers' home (our family friends of more than 20 years).

**SERVES 12**

12 large sweet potatoes

12 tablespoons unsalted butter, at room temperature

¾ cup firmly packed light brown sugar

¾ cup all-purpose flour

1 cup pecan pieces, toasted

1 cup miniature marshmallows

½ teaspoon salt

¼ teaspoon ground cinnamon

Preheat the oven to 400°F. Scrub the sweet potatoes and prick them with a fork in a couple of places. Place on a baking sheet. Bake for 45 to 50 minutes, until fork-tender.

Meanwhile, in a large bowl, mix the butter, brown sugar, and flour together until crumbly. Add the pecans, marshmallows, salt, and cinnamon. Stir to combine.

Slice the sweet potatoes lengthwise down the center and push the ends toward the middle to open them up. Stuff the potatoes with the streusel topping and return to the oven. Bake for another 20 minutes, or until the topping is bubbly and brown. Serve warm.

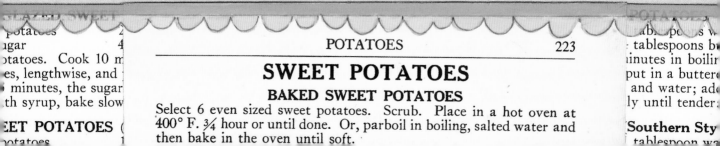

POTATOES     223

# SWEET POTATOES
## BAKED SWEET POTATOES

Select 6 even sized sweet potatoes. Scrub. Place in a hot oven at 400° F. ¾ hour or until done. Or, parboil in boiling, salted water and then bake in the oven until soft.

# Roasted Asparagus

In less than 15 minutes, you'll be serving up this tasty side dish!
The Parmesan cheese makes it a little more special.

**SERVES 4 TO 6**

1 pound asparagus, woody ends removed

Olive oil cooking spray

4 tablespoons unsalted butter, melted

½ cup grated Parmesan cheese

Juice of ½ lemon

Salt and freshly ground black pepper

Preheat the oven to 475°F.

Place the asparagus in a medium saucepan and cover with water. Bring to a boil and cook for 1 minute. Drain immediately and transfer to a small baking dish. Coat the asparagus with the olive oil spray and then drizzle with the melted butter. Scatter the Parmesan evenly over the top and roast for 7 to 8 minutes, until the cheese is melted. Remove from the oven and drizzle the lemon juice over all. Season with salt and pepper to taste and serve warm.

# KELSEY'S
# Asiago Au Gratin Potatoes

Asiago lovers, gather round! Although Kelsey Adams is young enough to be my daughter, I like to think of her as "the little sister of my heart." She shares my love of cooking and all things creative, which is why I asked her to share this dish with you. This recipe can be assembled, refrigerated, and covered several hours before baking. I garnish the dish with some fresh chives to add a little color.

### SERVES 6 TO 8

2 pounds medium Yukon gold potatoes

4 tablespoons unsalted butter

1 tablespoon all-purpose flour

1 teaspoon salt

2 cups whipping cream or half-and-half

2 cups shredded Asiago cheese

Chopped fresh chives, for garnish

In a medium saucepan, cover the whole potatoes with water. Bring to a boil over medium-high heat. Reduce the heat to medium and continue to boil until fork-tender, about 30 minutes. Drain the potatoes and set them aside to cool.

Meanwhile, in a medium saucepan, melt the butter over medium heat. Stir in the flour and salt. Cook, stirring constantly, until bubbly. Stir in the cream and continue stirring until the mixture comes to a boil. Boil and stir for 1 minute. Remove the cream mixture from the heat and stir in the cheese. Continue stirring until the cheese has melted.

Preheat the oven to 350°F. Butter a 13 by 9-inch casserole dish. Peel and slice the cooled potatoes. Alternately layer the potatoes and the sauce in the dish, finishing with the sauce. Bake uncovered until bubbly, about 30 minutes. Garnish with the chopped chives. Serve hot.

# Dee's Peas and Mushrooms

Dee Stoelting has contributed more recipes to my files than any other friend in the history of my cookbooks. She has managed a successful catering business for years. But she and her husband, Danny, are most famous for their countless acts of kindness in our community. I know you'll enjoy Dee's foolproof side dish—I like this with chicken, pork, or fish.

**SERVES 6 TO 8**

2 tablespoons unsalted butter

¼ cup thinly sliced scallions, white and green parts

1 cup sliced mushrooms of your choice

1 teaspoon sugar

½ teaspoon salt

⅛ teaspoon freshly ground black pepper

1 (10-ounce) bag frozen peas

In a large skillet, melt the butter of medium heat and sauté the scallions and mushrooms in the butter for 3 minutes, or until the scallions are soft. Add the sugar, salt, and pepper and stir. Add the peas and heat through. Serve warm.

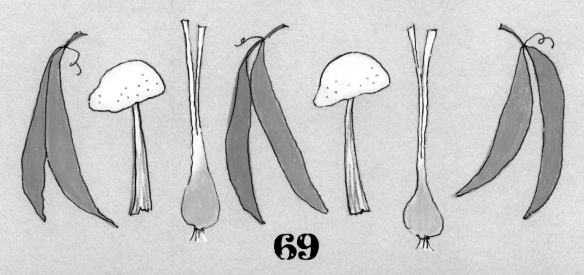

# Peach & Prosciutto Salad

In the summertime when fresh peaches are abundant, make sure you reserve a special place in your meal planning for this salad. The flavors are sweet and juicy and the presentation is flirtatious.

**SERVES 4**

¼ cup balsamic vinegar

2 tablespoons honey

2 fresh peaches, peeled, pitted, and cut into a total of 12 wedges

2 ounces thinly sliced prosciutto, cut into ½-inch strips

1 tablespoon olive oil

Salt and freshly ground black pepper

8 to 10 ounces spring lettuce mix

4 ounces Havarti cheese, sliced and then cut into ½-inch pieces

Chill 4 salad plates and a serving bowl.

Bring the vinegar to a boil in a small saucepan over medium-high heat. Decrease the heat and simmer until the vinegar is reduced to 2 tablespoons, about 2 minutes. Remove from the heat and stir in the honey. Set aside to cool to room temperature.

Spray a stovetop griddle or grill with nonstick cooking spray. Grill the peaches on the hot griddle for about 30 seconds, until grill marks appear. Remove from the griddle and set aside. Scatter the prosciutto on the griddle and cook until crisp.

Combine the oil and salt and pepper to taste in the chilled serving bowl. Mix well with a whisk. Add the lettuce and toss gently to coat. Top with the peach wedges and prosciutto. Drizzle the balsamic syrup over all. Scatter the cheese over the top and serve.

# White Cheddar Potato PANCAKES

I enjoy serving these as part of an evening meal as well as with breakfast or brunch. They may be prepared in advance and stored covered in the refrigerator for up to 1 week. Rewarm them at 350°F for 7 to 10 minutes.

### SERVES 4 TO 6

¼ cup chopped yellow onion

2 cups frozen hash brown potatoes

1 large egg, lightly beaten

½ teaspoon ground nutmeg

Salt and freshly ground black pepper

2 tablespoons olive oil

2 tablespoons salted butter

8 slices white cheddar cheese

Chopped fresh chives, for garnish

Combine the onion with the hash browns in a medium bowl. Add the egg, nutmeg, and salt and pepper. Mix well to coat the hash brown mixture.

Melt the oil and butter together on a griddle over medium-high heat. Using a ¼-cup dry measuring cup, scoop the potato mixture onto the hot griddle, flattening down lightly. Do not crowd the griddle. Top each pancake with a slice of cheese. Fry until crisp, about 4 minutes, and then carefully turn with a metal spatula so the cheese side is down. Cook for another 3 to 4 minutes, until the cheese is crisp. Transfer to a serving platter and keep warm while you finish cooking the pancakes. Garnish with chives and serve warm.

# Spiced Marinated Tomatoes

*This is a very refreshing salad: a little sweet, a little spicy, and very colorful. This is a good choice for picnics, buffets, and tailgating.*

**SERVES 4**

2 cups red and/or yellow cherry tomatoes, halved

¼ cup chopped red onion

½ cucumber, thinly sliced

2 cloves garlic, minced

¼ cup balsamic vinegar

1 tablespoon light brown sugar

1 tablespoon olive oil

Dash of Tabasco sauce

1 teaspoon peeled and minced fresh ginger

½ teaspoon seasoned salt

½ teaspoon seasoned pepper

¼ teaspoon ground cumin

Combine the tomatoes, red onion, cucumber, and garlic in a medium bowl.

In a small bowl, combine the vinegar, brown sugar, olive oil, Tabasco, ginger, salt, pepper, and cumin. Whisk until well blended. Pour the dressing over the tomato mixture and toss to coat. Chill for at least 1 hour before serving.

# Hazelnut Green Beans

When I see this recipe it brings back memories of living with the Chiles family during my last two years in high school. Mrs. Chiles didn't serve this particular dish, but she did introduce many different vegetables to me that I'd never tried before. She looked forward to receiving a package of fresh hazelnuts each fall from Oregon, where her father lived. She called them by another name, "filberts." If you have trouble finding hazelnuts, you may substitute walnuts with equally satisfying results.

### SERVES 4 TO 6

2 tablespoons salted butter, at room temperature

3 tablespoons finely chopped hazelnuts, toasted

1 teaspoon grated lemon zest

2 teaspoons salt

1½ pounds green beans, trimmed

Combine the butter, hazelnuts, lemon zest, and ½ teaspoon of the salt in a serving bowl. Blend with a fork.

Cover the green beans with water in a large saucepan. Add the remaining 1½ teaspoons salt and bring to a boil. Cook for 3 minutes. Drain the beans. Add the beans to the butter mixture and toss gently to coat. Serve warm.

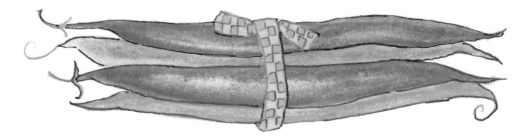

# Orange & Red Onion Salad

One of the blessings of this salad, the amazing fresh flavor aside, is the availability of the ingredients. When other fresh fruits are either too difficult to find or too expensive to serve, this is a bright alternative with a beautiful presentation. I have served this dish many times at catered breakfasts and lunches.

**SERVES 6**

8 navel oranges, peeled and sliced ¼ inch thick

½ red onion, thinly sliced

1 teaspoon salt

1 teaspoon sugar

½ teaspoon freshly ground black pepper

2 tablespoons olive oil

Arrange the orange slices in a single layer on a platter. Scatter the onion slices over all. Sprinkle with the salt, then the sugar, and finally with the pepper. Drizzle with the oil and serve.

# Chicken Caesar Pasta Salad

This recipe combines two of my favorite things—pasta salad and Caesar salad—into one dish. I like the blending of the two different textures of the pasta and the romaine. The addition of the pasta also makes it hearty enough to qualify as a main dish.

## SERVES 6

6 ounces penne, cooked according to package directions

3 cups sliced grilled chicken breast

2 cups thinly sliced romaine lettuce

1 cup grape tomatoes, halved

½ cup Caesar dressing

½ cup grated Parmesan cheese

Combine the pasta, chicken, romaine, tomatoes, dressing, and cheese in a large bowl. Toss to mix. Cover and refrigerate until ready to serve.

# Clarify

Today was a bad day in the kitchen. Just about every good idea I thought I had in regard to recipe testing turned out to be a disappointment. By 5:30 (one of my least favorite times in the winter, since the sun sets so early), I realized that I had used up the whole day, not to mention many expensive groceries, on dishes that, well, flopped. Darkness fell upon my already dark mood.

Desperate for springtime and sunshine, a long-ago image drifted into my thoughts. When I was about 13 years old, I had a poster in my bedroom of a little white flower that had pushed its way up through a tiny crack in a dirty city sidewalk. The caption on the poster read, "Beautiful things seldom come easy." As if to say: Clear the way, world—I will not let anything, including concrete and the filthy soles of an endless number of shoes, stand in my way of becoming what I was destined to become! My interpretation is a little dramatic, perhaps. But the point is, sometimes we have to push through some bad experiences to get to the really good ones. Clearly.

## CLARIFY: TO CLEAR A CLOUDY LIQUID BY REMOVING THE SEDIMENT

Breads

# Soft garlic breadsticks

I can't count the number of times someone has asked me to bring these breadsticks to a potluck gathering. They are melt-in-your-mouth good and very easy to prepare.

**MAKES 16 BREADSTICKS**

1¾ cups warm water

1 (.25-ounce) package quick-rise yeast

5 to 6 cups bread flour, plus more for rolling out

8 tablespoons unsalted butter, melted, plus 2 tablespoons
unsalted butter, at room temperature

2 tablespoons sugar

1 tablespoon plus 1 teaspoon sea salt

½ teaspoon garlic powder

¼ teaspoon dried oregano

½ cup shredded Parmesan cheese

Line two baking sheets with parchment paper.

Place ¼ cup of the water in the bowl of an electric mixer fitted with a dough hook. Add the yeast and mix well. Add 4 cups of the flour, the 2 tablespoons softened butter, sugar, 1 tablespoon of the salt, and the remaining 1½ cups water. Mix well. Continue adding the flour, a little at a time, until the dough pulls away from the sides of the bowl, about 5 minutes. Transfer to a floured surface and knead lightly until no longer sticky.

Roll the dough out into a 16 by 7-inch rectangle. Cut into 16 equal strips. Transfer the strips to the prepared baking sheets about 2 inches apart. Cover with a towel and allow to rise for about 30 minutes, until almost doubled.

Preheat the oven to 400°F. Combine the melted butter, the remaining 1 teaspoon salt, the garlic powder, and oregano in a small bowl. Brush the topping mixture over each breadstick and sprinkle with the Parmesan cheese. Reserve the extra topping mixture. Bake for about 15 minutes, or until light golden brown. Remove from the oven and brush the breadsticks with the remaining topping mixture before serving.

# Absurdly Cheesy Bread

Since this recipe makes two loaves, serve one warm with dinner and use the other one to make the most amazing grilled cheese sandwiches for lunch the next day. I have also used this bread to make tasty croutons to garnish soups and salads.

### MAKES TWO 9 BY 5-INCH LOAVES

2 cups milk

5 to 6 cups all-purpose flour

3 tablespoons sugar

1 teaspoon salt

2 (.25-ounce) packages quick-rise yeast

3 large eggs

1 pound cheddar cheese, shredded

Coat two 9 by 5 by 3-inch loaf pans with nonstick cooking spray and set aside. Warm the milk in the microwave for 1½ minutes.

In the bowl of an electric mixer fitted with a paddle attachment, mix together 2 cups of the flour, the sugar, salt, and yeast on low speed until combined. Add the milk and 2 of the eggs and beat for 2 minutes on medium speed. Switch the flat beater out for a dough hook attachment. Gradually add 3 cups of the flour and beat for 5 minutes. If the dough seems sticky, add up to 1 more cup flour and continue mixing until the dough begins to pull away from the side of the bowl.

Transfer the dough onto a lightly floured surface. Gradually knead the cheese into the dough. Divide the dough into two loaves and place in the prepared pans. Cover lightly with plastic wrap and let the dough rise for 45 minutes.

Preheat the oven to 375°F. In a small bowl, add a tablespoon of water to the remaining egg. Beat well and then brush over the tops of the loaves. Bake for 40 to 45 minutes, until lightly browned. Let cool in the pans for 10 minutes. Then turn the bread out onto a cooling rack.

# Pull-Apart Wheat Bread ♥

This recipe ranks in my top ten favorites of this collection. I'm so
impressed that such a simple list of ingredients can produce bread that
is so satisfying to the palate—and the presentation has star-like quality.
Once you try it, I think you'll be excited to share it with others too.

**SERVES 8 TO 10**

1¼ cups warm water

1 (.25-ounce) package quick-rise yeast

¼ cup packed light brown sugar

1½ teaspoons salt

2 large eggs

2 tablespoons salted butter, at room temperature,
plus 4 tablespoons salted butter, melted

2 cups wheat flour

3 to 4 cups all-purpose flour

Generously butter a 10-inch tube pan and also a medium bowl. Set aside.

In the bowl of an electric mixer fitted with a dough hook, combine the warm water, yeast, and brown sugar. Let stand until foamy, about 5 minutes. Add the salt, eggs, 2 tablespoons butter, and wheat flour. Beat well. Let rest for 10 minutes.

Add 2 cups of the all-purpose flour and continue beating. Slowly, to keep the mixture smooth, add 1 more cup of all-purpose flour to make a stiff dough. Let rest for 10 minutes.

Knead the dough (still in the mixer bowl fitted with the dough hook), gradually adding more all-purpose flour until the dough pulls away from the side of the mixer bowl. This should take 8 to 10 minutes. Place the dough in the prepared bowl and turn the buttered side up. Cover with a towel and let rise for 30 minutes, or until almost doubled.

Punch the dough down and turn onto a lightly floured surface. Divide the dough into quarters. Divide each quarter into quarters. Dip each of the 16 pieces into the melted butter and place in the prepared tube pan. Cover and let rise for 30 minutes, or until almost doubled.

Preheat the oven to 375°F. Bake the bread for 25 to 30 minutes, until a skewer inserted in the center of the loaf comes out clean. Cool in the pan for 5 minutes, then invert onto a serving platter.

# CRANBERRY WALNUT BREAKFAST BREAD

This bread is best enjoyed sliced and toasted with a generous amount of butter. I've also prepared it without the filling as a very nice option for sandwich bread.

**MAKES 2 LOAVES**

1 cup firmly packed light brown sugar

1 (.25-ounce) package quick-rise yeast

½ cup warm water

1 cup milk

12 tablespoons salted butter

3 large eggs, at room temperature

2 cups wheat flour

1 teaspoon salt

6 to 7 cups all-purpose flour

1 tablespoon ground cinnamon

1 cup walnuts, coarsely chopped

½ cup dried cranberries

Add 1 tablespoon of the brown sugar and the yeast to the warm water. Stir to dissolve and let rest until the water becomes foamy. Warm the milk and 8 tablespoons of the butter in a bowl in the microwave for 60 seconds on high power. Place the eggs, ½ cup of the brown sugar, the wheat flour, and salt in a mixing bowl. Add the yeast mixture and the milk-butter mixture to the mixing bowl. Using a dough hook attachment, mix all these ingredients well. Then gradually add the all-purpose flour until the dough begins to pull away from the sides of the bowl.

Coat a medium bowl with nonstick cooking spray. Transfer the dough to the bowl, turning the greased side up. Cover loosely with plastic wrap and allow to rise for 30 minutes, or until almost doubled.

In a small bowl, combine the remaining brown sugar and the cinnamon.

Coat two 9 by 5 by 3-inch loaf pans with nonstick cooking spray. Turn the dough out onto a lightly floured surface. Divide into two equal parts. Roll each part into a 10 by 8-inch rectangle. Spread each dough half with 2 tablespoons of the remaining butter. Sprinkle each with half the brown sugar mixture. Scatter the walnuts and cranberries over the top of the brown sugar mixture. Starting at the short end of the rectangle, roll up each dough half and place it seam side down in a prepared loaf pan. Cover each loaf lightly with plastic wrap and allow to rise for 30 minutes, or until almost doubled.

Preheat the oven to 375°F. Bake for 30 to 35 minutes, until golden brown. Allow the bread to cool in the loaf pans for 5 minutes before turning out onto wire racks to cool completely.

# Rosemary & Parmesan Focaccia

*This is a savory and sumptuous bread that comes together quickly.*

*I believe the cottage cheese is the secret ingredient!*

**SERVES 6 TO 8**

2 (.25-ounce) packages quick-rise yeast

½ cup warm water

1 cup small-curd cottage cheese

2 tablespoons sugar

1 tablespoon olive oil

2 tablespoons fresh rosemary
leaves, chopped

1 teaspoon salt

1 large egg

2½ to 3 cups all-purpose flour

Olive oil cooking spray

¼ cup shredded Parmesan cheese

In the large bowl of an electric mixer, dissolve the yeast in the warm water. Mash the cottage cheese with a fork in a glass measuring cup and warm the cottage cheese in the microwave for 30 seconds. Add the cottage cheese, sugar, olive oil, half of the rosemary, the salt, egg, and flour to the yeast mixture. Using a paddle attachment, mix well to make a stiff dough. Cover and let the dough rise in a warm place for 30 to 45 minutes, until doubled in bulk.

Spray a 13 by 9-inch baking dish with olive oil cooking spray. Spread the dough into the baking dish so that it covers the bottom completely. Spray the top with olive oil cooking spray and cover with plastic wrap. Let rise in a warm place for an additional 30 to 45 minutes, until doubled.

Preheat the oven to 375°F. Uncover the dough and sprinkle with the remaining rosemary. Scatter the cheese evenly over the top of the dough. Bake for 20 to 25 minutes, until golden. Serve warm.

# Orange Spice Muffins

If you're looking for a really moist breakfast muffin, these are just the solution.
As an added bonus, the batter may be kept in the refrigerator for up to
2 weeks, allowing you to bake small or large batches at the last minute.

### MAKES 3 DOZEN MUFFINS

1 cup salted butter, at
room temperature

2 cups sugar

2 large eggs

2 cups unsweetened applesauce

1 teaspoon orange extract

1 tablespoon ground cinnamon

1 teaspoon ground allspice

1 teaspoon ground nutmeg

4 cups all-purpose flour

2 teaspoons baking soda

1 teaspoon salt

36 pecan halves

Preheat the oven to 350°F. Line three muffin pans with paper liners.

In the large bowl of an electric mixer, beat the butter and sugar until fluffy.
Add the eggs and beat well. Stir in the applesauce, along with the orange
extract, cinnamon, allspice, and nutmeg. In a separate bowl, combine the
flour, baking soda, and salt. Fold the flour mixture into the wet ingredients,
stirring just until combined. Scoop the batter into the paper-lined muffin cups,
filling about two-thirds full. Place a pecan half centered on top of each muffin.

Bake for 15 to 18 minutes, until a wooden pick inserted in the center of a
muffin comes out clean. Let cool on a wire rack.

# Double Dark Chocolate Chip Muffins

These are my favorite muffins because I have the perfect excuse
to eat dessert for breakfast. I like finishing off half of the batch
with sliced almonds and leaving the other half plain.

**MAKES 15 MUFFINS**

8 tablespoons salted butter, softened

¾ cup granulated sugar

½ cup firmly packed light brown sugar

2 large eggs

⅔ cup sour cream

5 tablespoons milk

2 cups all-purpose flour

2 tablespoons unsweetened
dark cocoa powder

1 teaspoon baking soda

½ teaspoon salt

1¼ cups semisweet chocolate chips

½ cup sliced almonds (optional)

Powdered sugar, for garnish

Preheat the oven to 375°F. Line muffin pans with paper liners.

Cream together the butter, granulated sugar, and brown sugar. Add the eggs,
sour cream, and milk. Beat until well combined. In a separate bowl, mix together
the flour, cocoa powder, baking soda, and salt. Add the dry ingredients to the
wet ingredients and blend. Add the chocolate chips, mixing well.

Scoop the batter into the paper liners, filling about two-thirds full. Top with
the sliced almonds, if using. Bake for 22 to 24 minutes, until the center of
the muffins spring back when touched. Be careful not to overbake. Let cool
on a wire rack for 10 minutes. Dust with powdered sugar before serving.

# Brooke's Crisp Banana Waffles

My daughter made these for me on a Saturday morning when she was home for a Christmas vacation. She lined up a dozen different bowls of toppings, including a variety of fruits, nuts, and whipped cream, to create a "waffle bar." A beautiful presentation and an even more beautiful memory of her thoughtfulness.

**SERVES 4**

1 cup all-purpose flour

2 tablespoons sugar

2 teaspoons baking powder

½ teaspoon salt

¼ teaspoon ground cinnamon

¼ teaspoon ground nutmeg

2 large eggs, separated

1 cup milk

1 cup mashed bananas

6 tablespoons unsalted butter, melted

A variety of fresh fruits, chopped nuts, powdered sugar, whipped cream, and maple syrup, as desired, for serving

Blend the flour, sugar, baking powder, salt, cinnamon, and nutmeg together in a small bowl. In a medium bowl, beat the egg yolks and milk together. Add the flour mixture, stirring until just blended. Fold in the bananas and melted butter; mix well. In a small bowl, beat the egg whites until stiff peaks form. Gently fold the egg whites into the batter.

Preheat a waffle iron, and cook the waffles in batches following the manufacturer's instructions. To serve, finish with the toppings of your choice.

# ALMOND PANCAKES

When I asked my friend Jayne Wake if she had any new recipes to share for this book, she mentioned these pancakes enjoyed by her daughter, Jessi, at a recent "Cousins Weekend" in Lake Church, Michigan. Thanks, Jessi, one of my very favorite Iowa friends, for taking the time to share this with us!

### MAKES 12 TO 14 PANCAKES

1½ cups water

½ cup mascarpone cheese, at room temperature

1 tablespoon sugar

2 teaspoons almond extract

1 teaspoon vanilla extract

2 cups buttermilk pancake mix

4 ounces almond paste, cut into ¼-inch pieces

6 tablespoons unsalted butter, at room temperature

2 cups fresh raspberries

Maple syrup, for serving

In a food processor, combine the water, mascarpone, sugar, almond extract, and vanilla extract. Process until the mixture is smooth. Add the pancake mix and pulse until just combined. Add the almond paste pieces and pulse to incorporate.

Preheat a griddle over medium-low heat. Melt 1 tablespoon of butter on the griddle and, working in batches, pour ¼ cup of the batter per pancake onto the griddle. Cook for about 1½ minutes per side, until golden. Repeat with the remaining butter and batter. Serve warm with the raspberries and maple syrup.

# CaraMeLized onion FLatbread

This is quick! Don't you just love seeing that word at the beginning of a recipe from time to time? This flatbread has a good balance of sweet and savory flavors and is the perfect complement to a salad.

**SERVES 8 TO 10**

¼ cup olive oil

1 large or 2 medium yellow onions, thinly sliced

1 (13.8-ounce) roll refrigerated pizza dough

1 tablespoon sea salt

1 tablespoon chopped fresh rosemary

Preheat the oven to 425°F.

In a large skillet, heat 2 tablespoons of the oil over medium-high heat and sauté the onion for 8 to 10 minutes, stirring frequently, until golden.

Press the dough into a 15 by 10-inch jelly-roll pan, pressing to about a ¼-inch thickness. With the handle of a wooden spoon, make indentations in the dough every inch or so. Drizzle the remaining 2 tablespoons olive oil evenly over the top of the dough. Sprinkle with the salt, rosemary, and caramelized onion. Bake for 10 to 12 minutes, until golden brown. Let cool on a rack, then slice into squares and serve.

# Asiago Croutons

These are the perfect addition to the Creamy Tomato-Basil
Soup (page 36). You may also use them to top a favorite salad.
Leftovers will keep in an airtight container for up to 1 week.

## MAKES ABOUT 4 CUPS

Olive oil cooking spray

1 loaf French bread or Asiago cheese bread,
cut into 1-inch cubes

Sea salt

5 ounces Asiago cheese, shredded

Preheat the oven to 375°F. Spray a baking sheet with the olive oil cooking
spray. Transfer the bread cubes to the baking sheet. Spray the bread lightly
with olive oil cooking spray. Then sprinkle with salt. Scatter the cheese
evenly over the top. Bake for 8 to 10 minutes, until golden brown.

# Garlic Cheese Biscuits

We like these biscuits when fish is on the menu. The subtle garlic flavor seems like a nice complement to fish. But they also make a great little finger food when split and stuffed with a filling, like sliced ham or tomato or onion chutney.

**SERVES 4 TO 6**

2 cups biscuit baking mix (I use Bisquick)

⅔ cup milk

½ cup shredded cheddar cheese

All-purpose flour, for rolling out

4 tablespoons unsalted butter, melted

1 teaspoon minced garlic

Preheat the oven to 450°F. Coat a baking sheet with nonstick cooking spray.

In a large bowl, combine the biscuit mix, milk, and cheese and beat for about 30 seconds. Gently roll the dough out to a ½-inch thickness on a lightly floured surface. Cut into circles with a biscuit cutter (a drinking glass will also work if you don't have a biscuit cutter).

Place on the prepared baking sheet about 2 inches apart. Bake for 8 to 10 minutes, until golden brown. Transfer to a wire rack. Mix the butter and garlic together and brush the butter mixture over the warm biscuits.

# Caramel Rolls

If you have some extra space in your refrigerator, letting the rolls rise overnight is always a nice option. There is an overnight version listed at the end of the recipe. You may also substitute pecans for the walnuts, if you prefer.

**MAKES 24 ROLLS**

1 (18.25-ounce) package French vanilla cake mix

6 to 8 cups all-purpose flour

2 (.25-ounce) packages quick-rise yeast

1 teaspoon salt

2½ cups warm water (110 to 120°F)

1⅓ cups firmly packed light brown sugar

1½ cups salted butter

2 tablespoons light corn syrup

1½ cups chopped walnuts

¾ cup granulated sugar

1 tablespoon ground cinnamon

In the large bowl of an electric mixer, combine the dry cake mix, 2 cups of the flour, the yeast, and salt. Add the water and beat on low speed until combined. Then beat on high speed for 3 minutes.

Switch to a dough hook (or use a wooden spoon) and continue gradually adding 1 cup of flour at a time to make a smooth dough. This will take 3 to 5 minutes and the dough will still be slightly sticky. Then place the dough in a greased bowl. Turn the dough over with the greased side up. Cover and let rise in a warm place until doubled in size, about 30 minutes.

# BROWN SUGAR ❧ BUTTER ❧ WALNUTS ❧ SUGAR

While the dough is rising, combine the brown sugar, 1 cup of the butter, and the corn syrup in a heavy saucepan. Stir over medium heat until the mixture comes to a boil. Remove from the heat. Divide this mixture between two 13 by 9-inch baking dishes. Sprinkle each with the walnuts.

Punch the dough down. Turn out onto a well-floured surface and divide in half. Cover and let stand for 5 minutes. Then roll each portion into a 16 by 9-inch rectangle. Chop the remaining butter into small pieces and spread each rectangle with the butter. Combine the granulated sugar with the cinnamon and sprinkle over the dough.

Starting from the long side, roll up each dough piece, pinching to seal at the ends. Cut each of the rolls of dough into 12 slices. Place 12 pieces, cut side down, in each baking dish. Cover and let rise for about 45 minutes, or until almost doubled in size.

Preheat the oven to 350°F. Bake for 25 minutes, or until golden brown. Let cool on a wire rack for 10 minutes. Then turn out onto a pretty platter and serve.

### OVERNIGHT VERSION

Substitute 2 (.25-ounce) packages active dry yeast for the quick-rise yeast. Allow the dough to rise in the bowl (first rising) for 1 hour. After you have divided the punched-down dough into two pieces, let it stand for 10 minutes rather than 5 minutes. Finally, once you have placed the cut rolls into the baking dishes, cover and let rise in the refrigerator for up to 8 hours. About an hour before serving, remove the rolls from the refrigerator and let them rise in a warm place for about 30 minutes. Bake in a preheated oven as directed.

# CAKE MIX ❧ FLOUR ❧ YEAST ❧ SALT ❧ H₂O

# Orange Rolls

These rolls have just a hint of citrus, which makes them very complementary to a meal that includes fish or chicken. You may want to omit the glaze when serving in this way. They are also a good choice for brunch (with the glaze). The use of frozen bread dough (found in the freezer section of most grocery stores) will shorten your preparation time by at least 30 minutes.

## MAKES 1 DOZEN ROLLS

1 pound loaf frozen bread dough, thawed

Grated zest of 1 orange

½ cup granulated sugar

8 tablespoons salted butter, melted

### CITRUS GLAZE

1 cup powdered sugar

1 tablespoon salted butter, melted

3 tablespoons freshly squeezed orange juice

½ teaspoon vanilla extract

Coat a baking sheet with nonstick cooking spray. Cut the thawed dough into 12 equal pieces. Mix the orange zest with the granulated sugar. Dip each piece of dough into the melted butter and then into the sugar mixture. Place on the prepared baking sheet. Cover with plastic wrap and let rise in a warm place until doubled, about 45 minutes.

Preheat the oven to 350°F. Bake for 15 to 20 minutes, until golden brown. Transfer to a serving platter.

In a small bowl, combine all of the glaze ingredients, beating until smooth. Drizzle over the top of the warm rolls.

# PARMESAN FLATBREAD

This is such a simple recipe, but the bread adds a very nice touch when served on the side of a salad. You can vary the toppings, if you like. My favorite is described in this recipe, but you may substitute fresh chives, fresh rosemary, thinly sliced red onions, or a sprinkling of fresh thyme for the Parmesan.

### SERVES 10

1 (.25-ounce) package quick-rise yeast

1 cup warm water

3 cups all-purpose flour

3 tablespoons olive oil

1 tablespoon sugar

2 teaspoons sea salt, plus more for topping

1 large egg, beaten with 1 tablespoon water

Seasoned pepper

3 to 4 ounces Parmesan cheese, shaved

Sprinkle the yeast over the warm water in a medium bowl. Let rest for about 5 minutes, until the yeast is foamy. Add the flour, olive oil, sugar, and salt. Mix together until the ingredients form a ball. Knead lightly for about 2 minutes on a lightly floured surface, until the dough is smooth. Coat a medium bowl with oil and transfer the dough to the bowl, turning the dough over with the oiled side up. Cover the bowl and allow the dough to rise until doubled, 30 to 45 minutes.

Prepare three baking sheets by lining them with parchment paper. Preheat the oven to 350°F. Divide the dough into 10 equal pieces and roll each piece into a rectangle about 9 by 4 inches long. Transfer each piece to the prepared baking sheets, about 2 inches apart. Brush each piece with the egg wash. Sprinkle with salt, seasoned pepper, and cheese. Bake for 16 to 18 minutes, until golden brown. Let cool slightly on a wire rack before serving.

# Let Rest

There is a cooking term you've seen from time to time: let rest. Usually it relates to bread dough or sometimes meat. For instance, sometimes we are instructed to let cooked meat rest for a few minutes before carving, or to let bread dough rest before shaping. Take a breath. Pause. Rest.

There are dozens of situations in life when resting is just a grand idea in general. From naptime for little ones to the proverbial advice to "let sleeping dogs lie," we see the wisdom behind it. But what if we can't rest?

I won't go into all the phases of my life when a full night's sleep was impossible to come by. Sometimes it was when babies wouldn't sleep through the night. At other times for no apparent reason, my eyes would snap open in the wee hours of the morning as if they were spring-loaded. I would feel the impulse to solve every little problem in my life right then and there in the predawn darkness.

So, you'll understand why I had to purchase a cute little throw pillow I saw with this message stitched on it:

Sometimes I lie awake at night and wonder,
"Where did I go wrong?"
And then a little voice says to me,
"I'm pretty sure we're not going to be able
to cover this in just one night."

—(words by an American hero, Charlie Brown)

What a wise guy, that Charlie Brown.

Rest is Good

# desserts

# Zucchini Baby Cakes

I think of these as "big people" cupcakes, but not because children won't like them (they most certainly will!). It's because a typical cupcake brings a couple of images to mind: "room mother" and "children's parties." But you don't have to be one or attend the other in order to enjoy these.

**MAKES 24 CAKES**

3 cups all-purpose flour

1 teaspoon baking soda

½ teaspoon baking powder

1 teaspoon salt

2 teaspoons ground cinnamon

½ teaspoon ground nutmeg

1 cup vegetable oil

2 eggs, at room temperature

1 tablespoon vanilla extract

1 teaspoon grated lemon or orange zest

2 cups firmly packed light brown sugar

3 cups grated zucchini (about 2 medium)

Maple Cream Cheese Frosting (page 101)

Preheat the oven to 350°F. Line two muffin pans with paper liners.

In a medium bowl, whisk the flour, baking soda, baking powder, salt, cinnamon, and nutmeg together. In a large bowl, whisk together the oil, eggs, vanilla, and zest until well blended. Add the brown sugar and beat until smooth. Stir in the zucchini. Then add the flour mixture and stir just until combined.

Divide the batter evenly among the muffin cups, filling about two-thirds full. Bake until a tester inserted in the center of a muffin comes out clean, about 20 minutes. Cool completely on a wire rack before frosting.

# maple cream cheese frosting

*Besides being used on the Zucchini Baby Cakes, this frosting is also exceptionally good on the Pumpkin Cupcakes (page 110). It may also be used on any other cakes that make you think of autumn.*

**MAKES ABOUT 4 CUPS**

8 ounces cream cheese, at room temperature

4 tablespoons salted butter, at room temperature

1 teaspoon pure maple syrup

1 teaspoon vanilla extract

3 cups powdered sugar

In a bowl of an electric mixer fitted with a whip attachment, beat the cream cheese and butter until smooth. Stir in the maple syrup and vanilla. Add the powdered sugar gradually, beating on low speed, until smooth.

# Chocolate-Covered Banana Cheesecakes

This recipe makes about 16 individual cheesecakes, which are baked in oversize muffin pans. I created this recipe for a friend's bridal shower because I wanted individual cakes that wouldn't require one of us to be in the kitchen at the last minute, struggling with slicing and garnishing a large cheesecake. I was able to garnish the individual cheesecakes before everyone arrived. The little cakes still looked beautiful after sitting on the buffet table for an hour, while we finished our main course. They were a big hit!

**SERVES 16**

24 cream-filled vanilla sandwich cookies, crushed in a food processor

4 tablespoons salted butter, melted

24 ounces cream cheese, at room temperature

⅔ cup granulated sugar

2 tablespoons cornstarch

3 large eggs

1 cup mashed bananas

2½ cups Hour Power Whipped Cream (page 142)

1 cup Hazelnut Fudge Confection Sauce (page 104) or Chocolate Ganache (page 131)

Chocolate sprinkles, for garnish

Preheat the oven to 350°F. In a small bowl, combine the crushed cookies with the melted butter. Blend well. Line 16 oversized muffin cups and add a heaping tablespoon of this mixture to each cup. Press the crumb mixture lightly into the bottom of each liner.

In the bowl of an electric mixer fitted with a paddle attachment, beat the cream cheese until smooth and creamy. Beat in the granulated sugar and cornstarch, followed by the eggs, one at a time. Beat in the bananas, ½ cup of the heavy cream, and the vanilla until well combined. Distribute the mixture evenly between the 16 muffin cups.

Bake for 15 minutes. Reduce the oven temperature to 200°F and bake for an additional 40 minutes. Turn off the oven and open the oven door slightly, leaving the cheesecakes in the oven for an additional 30 minutes.

Remove the cakes from the oven and allow them to cool at room temperature for 1 hour. Carefully remove them from the muffin pans and place on a large platter in the refrigerator. Do not cover the cakes. Refrigerate overnight.

About an hour before serving, prepare the Hour Power Whipped Cream. Top each cheesecake with a generous spoonful of the chocolate filling. Then follow with two generous spoonfuls of the whipped topping. Garnish with chocolate sprinkles and arrange on a platter to serve.

# Hazelnut Fudge Confection Sauce

This decadent dessert sauce is used in the Chocolate-Covered Banana Cheesecakes (page 102), but it is also wonderful served warm over ice cream or as a fruit dip. I have divided the recipe into small jars and given the sauce as a gift for special occasions. Store the sauce in the refrigerator for up to 2 weeks.

**MAKES ABOUT 4 CUPS**

1½ cups semisweet or dark chocolate chips

8 tablespoons salted butter

½ cup Nutella

1⅓ cups sugar

1⅓ cups evaporated milk

In a small heavy saucepan, melt the chocolate, butter, and Nutella over medium heat. Add the sugar. Then gradually stir in the evaporated milk. Stir frequently and bring to a boil. Reduce the heat to low and boil gently for 8 minutes, stirring frequently.

Remove the sauce from the heat to cool. Ladle into an airtight container or multiple jars and store in the refrigerator until ready to use. When ready to serve, warm the sauce in the microwave in 30-second intervals, stirring in between, until warm.

# pumpkin gooey butter cake

This simple but luscious treat may be served as a coffee cake or dessert. I've also made individual cakes in paper-lined muffin cups with equal success. Just make sure to decrease the baking time by 5 to 10 minutes when baking small-size cakes. My favorite way to serve this cake is with a scoop of cinnamon ice cream on the side.

**SERVES 10 TO 12**

1 cup salted butter

1 (18.25-ounce) package
yellow cake mix

1 large egg

8 ounces cream cheese,
at room temperature

1 cup canned solid-pack pumpkin puree

1 (16-ounce) box powdered
sugar, plus more for garnish

Preheat the oven to 350°F. In a medium bowl, melt ½ cup of the butter on high power in the microwave. Add the contents of the yellow cake mix and the egg. Mix until well blended. Transfer this mixture to a 13 by 9-inch baking dish, pressing the dough to distribute it evenly over the bottom of the dish.

Melt the remaining ½ cup butter in a small bowl in the microwave. Blend the cream cheese and pumpkin together in a separate bowl until smooth. Add the melted butter and continue to mix. Add the powdered sugar and blend until creamy. Pour this mixture over the dough in the bottom of the baking dish and bake until set, 35 to 40 minutes. The edges of the cake will be only light golden brown. Cool on a wire rack for about 1 hour. Garnish with a dusting of powdered sugar and serve.

# Cheese-Filled Chocolate Bundt Cake

If there is one dessert that almost always makes me happy, it's one with the word chocolate in the title. This cake has an interesting, almost fudge-brownie-like texture, with a rich tunnel of cream cheese filling running through it (only adding to my bliss).

**SERVES 10 TO 12**

8 ounces cream cheese, at room temperature

2¼ cups granulated sugar

1 teaspoon vanilla extract

3 large eggs

1 cup semisweet chocolate chips

1 cup vegetable oil

1 teaspoon vanilla extract

3 cups all-purpose flour

⅔ cup unsweetened cocoa powder

2 teaspoons baking soda

½ teaspoon salt

¼ cup dry cultured buttermilk (found in the baking aisle of the grocery store)

1 cup water

¼ cup powdered sugar, for garnish

Preheat the oven to 325°F. Coat a Bundt or tube pan with nonstick cooking spray and dust with a little flour. Set aside.

For the filling, in the bowl of an electric mixer, beat the cream cheese, ¼ cup of the granulated sugar, and vanilla until smooth. Add 1 of the eggs and continue beating until well incorporated. Stir in the chocolate chips.

In the large bowl using the electric mixer, beat the 2 remaining eggs, the remaining 2 cups granulated sugar, oil, and vanilla until thick and smooth. In another bowl, combine the flour, cocoa, baking soda, salt, and dry buttermilk. Add half of the dry ingredients to the creamed mixture and mix well. Add half of the water and continue mixing. Repeat with the remaining dry ingredients and the remaining water. Beat until smooth. Spoon half of the batter into the prepared pan. Spoon the cream cheese filling on top of this. Add the remaining cake batter over the cream cheese filling.

Bake for 1 hour and 15 minutes, or until a cake tester inserted in the middle comes out clean. Let the cake cool in the pan for about 15 minutes before inverting it onto a plate. Let cool completely before slicing. Dust lightly with the powdered sugar to garnish.

# Hummingbird CAKE

This past summer I hosted a bridal shower for one of my favorite young friends. I was looking for a dessert recipe that had a vintage feel, since the bride loved that particular style. Although I'm not sure 1978 would qualify as "vintage" (which is when Hummingbird Cake first appeared on the scene), the recipe was at least 10 years older than the bride. So we went with it, and it did indeed take us back to a sweet simpler time. Dress your friends up in vintage aprons, and don't forget to wear your pearls.

### SERVES 10 TO 12

**CAKE**

3 cups all-purpose flour

2 cups sugar

1 teaspoon salt

1 teaspoon baking soda

1 teaspoon ground cinnamon

3 large eggs, beaten

1½ cups vegetable oil

1½ teaspoons vanilla extract

1 (8-ounce) can crushed pineapple

2 cups chopped pecans

2 cups mashed overripe bananas

**CREAM CHEESE FROSTING**

1 pound cream cheese, at room temperature

1 cup salted butter, at room temperature

1 (2-pound) package powdered sugar

2 teaspoons vanilla extract

Preheat the oven to 350°F. Coat three 9-inch round cake pans with nonstick cooking spray, and line each with a circle of parchment paper on the bottom only.

To make the cake, combine the flour, sugar, salt, baking soda, and cinnamon in a large mixing bowl. Add the eggs and oil, stirring just until moistened. Stir in the vanilla, pineapple, 1 cup of the pecans, and the bananas. Divide the batter evenly between the three prepared pans. Bake for 25 to 30 minutes, until a tester inserted in the center of each pan comes out clean. Let cool completely before frosting.

To make the frosting, combine the cream cheese and butter in the bowl of an electric mixer fitted with a paddle attachment, blending well. Add the powdered sugar gradually and continue beating until smooth and creamy. Add the vanilla and mix well. Frost the cake and then decorate it with the remaining 1 cup pecans, pressing them into the top and sides.

HUMMINGBIRD CAKE

# PumPKin
## cupcakes

This is the most popular cupcake we make at the Paint Box Café. I like making these in miniature size so that I can have one a day, guilt free, until they're all gone. If you like, frost with Maple Cream Cheese Frosting (page 101).

MAKES 10 REGULAR OR
24 MINIATURE CUPCAKES

1 cup plus 2 tablespoons all-purpose flour

1 teaspoon baking powder

½ teaspoon baking soda

½ teaspoon salt

1 teaspoon ground cinnamon

½ teaspoon ground ginger

½ teaspoon ground nutmeg

3 large eggs, at room temperature

1 cup canned solid-pack pumpkin puree

½ cup granulated sugar

½ cup firmly packed light brown sugar

½ cup vegetable oil

Preheat the oven to 350°F. Line a muffin pan (or two mini muffin pans) with paper liners. In a medium bowl, stir together the flour, baking powder, baking soda, salt, cinnamon, ginger, and nutmeg. In a bowl of an electric mixer, beat together the eggs, pumpkin, sugars, and vegetable oil. Add the flour mixture and mix until combined.

Divide the batter evenly among the paper liners and bake for 20 to 25 minutes for the regular cakes (16 to 18 minutes for the mini cakes). A toothpick, when inserted in the center, should come out clean. Let cool completely.

# CRANAPPLE PIE

I'm sure I can't prove this, but I would swear that the crisp autumn air actually causes some kind of biological reaction within me, resulting in a craving for desserts stuffed with either cranberries or apples. With this recipe I can have both! I like this pie with a scoop of cinnamon or vanilla ice cream on top.

**SERVES 8**

One (15-ounce) package rolled refrigerated piecrusts

2 tablespoons freshly squeezed orange or lemon juice

1 teaspoon orange extract

5 medium tart apples (such as Granny Smith),
peeled, cored, and sliced

1 cup fresh or frozen cranberries

1 cup broken walnuts

¾ cup sugar

2 tablespoons all-purpose flour

1 teaspoon ground cinnamon

⅛ teaspoon ground nutmeg

Preheat the oven to 375°F. Ease one of the refrigerated piecrusts into a 9-inch pie plate. Place the orange juice and orange extract in a medium bowl. Add the apples, cranberries, walnuts, sugar, flour, cinnamon, and nutmeg. Toss until well combined, and then arrange the filling in the pie plate. Top with the second piecrust and crimp the edges as desired. Bake for 50 minutes, or until the crust is golden brown. Let cool on a wire rack.

# Paradise Pie

This is the kind of dessert you'd eat while on vacation. It's just that special. It's a very dense cake-and-pie combination that always gets a big reaction from guests. Dig in!

**SERVES 10 TO 12**

8 tablespoons salted butter

1 cup graham cracker crumbs

1 cup sugar

1½ cups chocolate chips

1 cup all-purpose flour

1½ teaspoons baking powder

⅔ cup half-and-half

2 tablespoons vegetable oil

2 teaspoons vanilla extract

⅔ cup chocolate chips

½ cup unsweetened shredded coconut

½ cup pecans or walnuts, finely chopped

Vanilla ice cream, for serving

Hazelnut Fudge Confection Sauce (page 104) or Chocolate Ganache (page 131), for serving

Preheat the oven to 350°F. For the crust, melt the butter in a medium bowl in the microwave. Add the graham cracker crumbs and ½ cup of the sugar and mix well. Press into the bottom of a 2-quart baking dish. (I like using a round or oval dish for this recipe.) Top with the chocolate chips and bake for 5 minutes. Spread the melted chips evenly over the crust.

In a large bowl, combine the flour, the remaining ½ cup sugar, and the baking powder. Add the half-and-half, oil, and vanilla and mix until smooth. Stir in the chocolate chips, coconut, and nuts. Pour into the crust.

Bake for 35 to 40 minutes, until a tester inserted in the center comes out clean. Serve warm with ice cream and your choice of chocolate sauces.

# Deep Dark Brownie Pie

If you're ever wondering what to prepare when you're craving cookies, brownies, and pie all at the same time, this is it. The combination of textures and flavor ranks way up there with your wildest dessert fantasies. Chewy, nutty crust; creamy, decadent filling; and chocolate perfection. If you're in a hurry, you may substitute whipped cream in place of the Chocolate Ganache.

**SERVES 8**

1 cup salted butter, at room temperature

1 cup all-purpose flour

1½ cups sugar

½ cup chopped pecans

2 (1-ounce) squares unsweetened chocolate

⅔ cup semisweet chocolate chips

2 large eggs

1 teaspoon vanilla extract

1 cup all-purpose flour

½ teaspoon baking powder

½ teaspoon salt

1 cup Chocolate Ganache
(page 131), for serving

Preheat the oven to 325°F. For the crust, combine ½ cup of the butter, the flour, ¼ cup of the sugar, and the pecans in a medium bowl. Mix until crumbly. Press this mixture into the bottom and up the sides of a 9-inch pie plate. Set aside.

Combine the unsweetened chocolate and chocolate chips with the remaining ½ cup butter in a medium bowl. Microwave for 45 to 60 seconds, until the chocolate is almost melted. Remove and stir until the chocolate is melted completely. Whisk in the remaining 1¼ cups sugar. Then add the eggs, one at a time, mixing well after each addition. Blend in the vanilla.

In a small bowl, whisk together the flour, baking powder, and salt. Blend into the chocolate mixture just until incorporated. Transfer the chocolate filling into the piecrust. Bake for 40 to 45 minutes, until set in the center. Let cool for at least 2 hours before serving.

To serve, cut the pie into wedges and finish each slice with a drizzle of Chocolate Ganache.

# over the moon SILVER SPOONS

This chocolate-dipped spoon makes a sweet party favor or a great care package component. Line them up on a dessert table at a shower or tuck them into a basket filled with cocoa mix and coffee beans for a hostess gift. I buy the most inexpensive stainless-steel spoons I can find at a discount store, rather than using plastic spoons.

### MAKES 15 SPOONS

⅔ cup semisweet chocolate chips

2 ounces Baker's white chocolate

Chocolate or pastel sprinkles (optional)

Lay waxed paper or parchment paper on a flat surface. This is where you will be allowing the chocolate-covered spoons to dry.

In a small bowl, melt the chocolate chips on high power in the microwave, stirring every 30 seconds, until smooth. This shouldn't take more than 60 to 90 seconds.

Dip each spoon into the melted chocolate, covering the bowl of the spoon up to the bottom of the handle. Gently shake the excess chocolate off the spoon and lay on the prepared sheet of paper. Repeat with all the spoons.

In a freezer-safe resealable plastic bag, melt the white chocolate in the microwave on high power for 30 seconds at a time until melted. Massage the bag after the first 30 seconds to help distribute the heat and evenly melt the chocolate. Be careful not to scorch. Cut off a tiny tip at the corner of the bag and drizzle the white chocolate back and forth across the semisweet chocolate in a decorative pattern. Scatter the sprinkles, if using, over the spoons. Leave to dry for at least 30 to 60 minutes. You may speed up the drying process by placing the spoons in the refrigerator. When completely dry, place each spoon inside a small cellophane bag and tie with a ribbon. Store at room temperature.

# Peanut Butter-Chocolate Fudge Cups

If you're interested in a cute idea for a party favor, try these decadent treats.
I found the individual silicone baking cups at a hobby store in the baking
supply aisle. Small cellophane bags may be used to package each individual
fudge cup. Just tie the bag closed with a ribbon and you're done!

**MAKES 12**

½ cup evaporated milk

1½ cups sugar

Pinch of salt

1 teaspoon salted butter

¼ teaspoon vanilla extract

1 cup creamy peanut butter

½ cup chocolate chips

In a medium saucepan, combine the evaporated milk, sugar, and salt. Cook over
medium heat for about 10 minutes. Turn off the heat and add the butter, vanilla, and
peanut butter, blending well.

Place the baking cups on a tray. Distribute the peanut butter mixture equally among the
baking cups. Sprinkle a few chocolate chips on top of the peanut butter mixture in the
cups. You may leave the chips whole, or swirl slightly with the back of a spoon. Place the
tray of cups in the refrigerator for at least 45 minutes before storing or packaging.

# Apple Turnovers

These light and delicate turnovers come together quickly using the Spiced Apples as the filling. The frozen puff pastry makes this recipe so easy. What you don't eat at breakfast or brunch would be incredible nestled next to a scoop of ice cream for dessert.

**SERVES 12**

All-purpose flour, for rolling out dough

2 sheets frozen puff pastry, thawed

1 recipe Spiced Apples (page 59)

1 large egg, beaten with 1 tablespoon water

Powdered sugar, for garnish

Preheat the oven to 425°F. Line two baking sheets with parchment paper. Scatter flour over a clean work surface. Roll out each sheet of pastry on the floured surface into a 9 by 6-inch rectangle. Cut each sheet into 6 equal squares.

Lay the pastry squares on the parchment paper, at least a few inches apart. Spoon about ¼ cup of the spiced apple filling onto the center of each square. Fold the pastry over the filling to form a triangle. Seal the edges with a fork. Brush the egg wash over the top of each triangle. Bake for 12 to 14 minutes, until golden brown. Let cool on a wire rack for at least 10 minutes. Dust with powdered sugar before serving.

# Roxie's Favorite
## ONE-BOWL CHOCOLATE CHIP COOKIES

I tried a version of this recipe and found that by adding coconut to it,
it became my very favorite chocolate chip cookie recipe of all time.
What makes it even more favorable is the whole one-bowl deal.

### MAKES 3 DOZEN COOKIES

1 cup salted butter

¾ cup firmly packed light brown sugar

¾ cup granulated sugar

1 teaspoon salt

2 teaspoons vanilla extract

2 large eggs

2⅓ cups all-purpose flour

½ teaspoon baking soda

¼ teaspoon baking powder

2 cups semisweet chocolate chips

1 cup walnuts or pecans (optional)

1 cup unsweetened shredded coconut

Preheat the oven to 350°F.

In a large bowl, melt the butter on high power in the microwave. This will
take about 60 seconds. Stir both sugars into the melted butter. Add the salt,
vanilla, and eggs and mix until well combined. Add the flour, baking soda,
and baking powder and mix well. Fold in the chocolate chips, nuts, if using,
and coconut. Chill the dough for about 20 minutes.

Scoop out the dough with a 1½-inch cookie scoop onto ungreased baking
sheets, spacing the dough about 2 inches apart. Bake for 12 to 13 minutes, until
golden brown. Let cool on a wire rack.

# Peanut Butter Dreams

This is a luscious sandwich cookie! Don't be surprised if your friends and family members request them often. Fortunately, the ingredients are pretty standard fare, usually stocked in my cupboard.

### MAKES ABOUT 30 COOKIES

2 cups all-purpose flour

1½ teaspoons baking soda

½ teaspoon salt

1 cup salted butter, at room temperature

2 cups creamy peanut butter

1½ cups granulated sugar

1 cup firmly packed light brown sugar

2 large eggs

2 teaspoons vanilla extract

8 ounces cream cheese, at room temperature

¾ cup creamy peanut butter

¾ cup powdered sugar

Preheat the oven to 350°F. Line two baking sheets with parchment paper.

In a medium bowl, whisk together the flour, baking soda, and salt. In the larger bowl of an electric mixer, cream together the butter, peanut butter, 1 cup of the granulated sugar, and the brown sugar. Beat in the eggs and vanilla until well incorporated. Then gently fold in the flour mixture.

Scoop out the dough with a 1½-inch cookie scoop onto the baking sheets, spacing the dough about 2 inches apart. Then sprinkle the remaining ½ cup granulated sugar over each scoop of dough. Using a fork dipped in sugar, press each dough ball gently to make a crisscross pattern. Bake for 10 to 12 minutes. Let cool on wire racks for at least 5 minutes.

To make the filling, blend the cream cheese and peanut butter together in a medium bowl until smooth. Then beat in the powdered sugar until creamy.

When the cookies are completely cool, spread the bottom side of a cookie with the filling and top with the flat side of another cookie, so that the crisscross pattern shows on the top and the bottom. Press together lightly and repeat until all the cookies are filled.

# Salted Chocolate COOKIES

Earlier this year, I discovered a chocolate bar that featured dark chocolate, panko (a type of bread crumbs), and sea salt. It was surprising how this simple combination of ingredients could be so rich in flavor. So I tried creating a cookie that echoed these flavors. The broken pecan pieces add a nice crunch.

## MAKES ABOUT 2 DOZEN COOKIES

8 ounces semisweet chocolate

¾ cup firmly packed light brown sugar

4 tablespoons salted butter,
at room temperature

2 large eggs

1 teaspoon vanilla extract

½ cup all-purpose flour

¼ teaspoon baking powder

2 cups semisweet chocolate chips

2 cups broken pecan pieces

3 to 4 teaspoons coarse sea salt

¼ cup panko bread crumbs

Preheat the oven to 350°F. Line two baking sheets with parchment paper.

In a large bowl, melt the baking chocolate squares in the microwave on high power for about 90 seconds. Stir until the chocolate is melted and smooth. Add the brown sugar, butter, eggs, and vanilla. Mix until well combined. Stir in the flour and baking powder. Fold in the chocolate chips and pecans.

Scoop out the dough with a 1½-inch cookie scoop onto the baking sheets, spacing the dough about 2 inches apart. Flatten each ball of dough slightly. Sprinkle each scoop of cookie dough with some sea salt and a little bit of the panko. Bake for 10 to 12 minutes. Let cool on the cookie sheets until set for at least 5 minutes before serving.

# LuLus

This cookie can be found in our bakery case each day at the Paint Box Café. It is a cross between a peanut butter, an oatmeal, and a chocolate chip cookie. I named them LuLus for "short." You may store the dough in the refrigerator for up to 2 weeks, baking only what you need for the moment.

### MAKES ABOUT 4 DOZEN COOKIES

3 cups all-purpose flour

1 tablespoon baking soda

¾ teaspoon salt

¾ teaspoon ground cinnamon

1½ cups salted butter, at room temperature

1½ cups creamy peanut butter

1½ cups granulated sugar

1½ cups light brown sugar

1½ teaspoons vanilla extract

3 large eggs, at room temperature

2¼ cups quick-cooking rolled oats

1½ cups semisweet chocolate chips

1½ cups dark chocolate chips

Whisk together the flour, baking soda, salt, and cinnamon.

In the bowl of an electric mixer fitted with a paddle attachment, cream together the butter, peanut butter, granulated sugar, brown sugar, and vanilla on medium speed. Add the eggs and beat to combine. On low speed, gradually add the flour mixture until just combined. Stir in the oats and chocolate chips. Chill the dough for at least 3 hours.

Preheat the oven to 350°F. Line baking sheets with parchment paper.

Use a small ice cream scoop or your hands to form about 3 tablespoons of dough. Scoop out the dough in 3-tablespoon portions with a small ice cream scoop or your hands onto the baking sheets, spacing the dough about 2 inches apart. Bake for 10 minutes, or until the cookies are lightly golden. The cookies should appear slightly underbaked when you take them out of the oven. Let cool on a wire rack.

# Lush Lemon Bars

I think you'll enjoy this recipe for so many reasons. It takes very little time to assemble and can be garnished in a variety of ways to make a spectacular presentation. It's also a great make-ahead dessert and can be stored in the refrigerator for several days until you need it. The texture is both creamy and crispy, thanks to the lemon curd filling and the coconut-almond topping.

**SERVES 20**

1 cup salted butter, at room temperature

1 cup sugar

2 cups all-purpose flour

½ teaspoon baking powder

¼ teaspoon salt

1 (10- to 12-ounce) jar lemon curd

1 cup unsweetened shredded coconut

⅔ cup sliced almonds

10 fresh strawberries or
1¼ cups cherry pie filling,
for garnish

Preheat the oven to 375°F.

In the large bowl of an electric mixer using a paddle attachment, beat the butter on medium speed for about 30 seconds. Add the sugar and beat just until combined. Add the flour, baking powder, and salt. Beat until just combined and the mixture looks like coarse crumbs. Reserve ⅔ cup of the crumb mixture. Press the remaining crumb mixture into the bottom of a 13 by 9-inch baking dish. Bake for 7 to 8 minutes, until the top is golden. Remove from the oven.

Spread the lemon curd gently over the top of the hot crust to within ½ inch of the outside edge.

In a medium bowl, combine the reserved crumb mixture with the coconut and almonds. Scatter this over the top of the lemon curd. Return to the oven and bake for an additional 18 to 20 minutes, until golden brown. Let cool for about 10 minutes on a wire rack.

Cut into 20 bars and garnish each with a fresh strawberry half or 1 tablespoon of cherry pie filling. (If you aren't serving them right away, garnish them right before serving.)

# Tahiti Sweetie Cookie Mix

This cookie mix makes a great gift, especially when presented in a clear canister, showing off the layers and layers of goodness inside. Tie the recipe instructions to the lid with a ribbon, and—ta-da!—no extra gift wrapping required.

**MAKES 30 COOKIES**

½ cup granulated sugar

½ cup chopped hazelnuts or pecans

1¼ cups unsweetened shredded coconut

1 cup crushed cornflakes

¾ cup firmly packed light brown sugar

½ cup quick-cooking rolled oats

1¼ cups all-purpose flour

1 teaspoon baking soda

1 teaspoon baking powder

¼ teaspoon salt

To assemble the mix, it's helpful to use a widemouthed funnel for filling the container to keep the layers "clean" looking. Make sure the canister you're filling holds at least 6 cups. Begin layering with the sugar, then the nuts, coconut, crushed cornflakes, brown sugar, and oats. In a small bowl, mix together the flour, baking soda, baking powder, and salt. Add this mixture to the jar. Cover with the lid.

**FOR THE NOTE CARD**

To prepare the cookies, preheat the oven to 350°F. Line two baking sheets with parchment paper. In the bowl of an electric mixer, stir together the contents of the container. Add 8 tablespoons softened salted butter, 1 beaten egg, and 1 teaspoon vanilla extract. Mix on low speed until the dough is well combined and pulls away from the sides of the bowl.

Scoop out the dough with a 1½-inch cookie scoop onto the baking sheets, spacing the dough about 2 inches apart. Bake for 10 to 12 minutes, until light golden brown. Let cool for at least 2 minutes on the baking sheets before serving.

6 Cup Canister →

Large Mouth Funnel ↓

DiRecTioNs

# Turtle Shortbread Bars

I like including this bar when creating a platter of assorted cookies. It can be cut into squares, rectangles, or diamond shapes, and the layered look adds great visual interest. For extra fun, you can top each bar with a glazed pecan. There is a good recipe for glazed pecans in my book *At Our Table*.

**SERVES 10 TO 12**

### SHORTBREAD LAYER

4 tablespoons salted butter, at room temperature

1¼ cups all-purpose flour

¼ cup sugar

½ cup finely chopped pecans

### FILLING

1 cup salted butter

½ cup sugar

3 tablespoons dark corn syrup

1 (14-ounce) can sweetened condensed milk

### TOPPING

1 cup dark chocolate chips

Preheat the oven to 350°F. Coat a 10 by 7-inch baking dish or pan with nonstick cooking spray. Then line the pan with two pieces of parchment paper, large enough to overlap the pan edges on all four sides.

To make the shortbread layer, combine the butter, flour, sugar, and pecans in a bowl and beat until well combined. Press the mixture evenly into the prepared pan. Bake for 18 to 22 minutes, until light golden brown.

To make the filling, heat the butter, sugar, corn syrup, and condensed milk in a medium saucepan over low heat. Stir often until combined and then bring to a boil over medium-high heat. Decrease the heat and simmer for 8 to 10 minutes, stirring constantly, until the mixture becomes thick. Pour this mixture over the shortbread and refrigerate until firm.

To make the topping, melt the chocolate chips in a glass measuring cup in the microwave, heating them in 30-second intervals and stirring after each interval. This should take only 60 to 90 seconds. Pour the melted chocolate over the filling and return to the refrigerator for 1 hour. Slice into bars.

# Dee's Sugar Cookies

My friend of more than 35 years, Dee Stoelting, shares this recipe with us. Besides my sister, Jan, Dee is the only person who has had a recipe featured in every cookbook I've ever created. Her daughter, Dana, uses this recipe as a base for her Caramel Apple Cookies (page 129).

## MAKES ABOUT 30 DOZEN COOKIES

½ cup vegetable shortening

4 tablespoons salted butter, at room temperature

1½ cups sugar

2 large eggs

5 tablespoons milk

1 teaspoon vanilla extract

4 cups all-purpose flour

1 teaspoon baking powder

1 teaspoon baking soda

½ teaspoon salt

In a medium bowl, cream together the shortening, butter, and sugar until light and fluffy. Add the eggs and mix well. In a small bowl, combine the milk and vanilla. In a separate bowl, mix the flour, baking powder, baking soda, and salt. Add the milk mixture alternately with the flour mixture to the creamed mixture until well combined. Chill the dough for at least 20 minutes.

Preheat the oven to 375°F. Line two baking sheets with parchment paper. Roll out the dough on a lightly floured surface to a ⅛-inch thickness and cut into desired shapes. Arrange the cut cookie dough about 2 inches apart on the prepared pans. Bake for 8 to 10 minutes, until the edges are light brown. Transfer the cookies immediately to a wire rack to cool.

·GOOD FRIENDS·GOOD FOOD·GOOD TIMES·

# DANA'S Caramel Apple Cookies

My friend Dana Becker makes this recipe using her mom's sugar cookies or a peanut butter cookie as the base. See Dee's Sugar Cookies (page 128), or use the Peanut Butter Dreams cookie recipe on page 118 (without the cream filling).

### MAKES 2 DOZEN COOKIES

8 ounces cream cheese, at room temperature

½ cup firmly packed light brown sugar

¼ cup creamy peanut butter

1 teaspoon vanilla extract

24 homemade sugar or peanut butter cookies

2 tart apples, such as Granny Smith, peeled, cored, and diced

½ cup lemon-lime soda or 2 tablespoons freshly squeezed lemon juice

¼ cup caramel ice cream topping

2 regular-size Snickers bars, chopped (optional)

In the bowl of an electric mixer, beat the cream cheese until smooth. Add the brown sugar and mix well. Blend in the peanut butter and vanilla. Spread each cookie with the cream cheese mixture.

Toss the diced apples in the soda to prevent them from turning brown. Drain off the liquid. Distribute the apples over the top of the cream cheese mixture on each cookie. Drizzle the caramel topping over the tops of the apples. Press bits of the chopped candy bars, if using, into the tops of the cookies. Refrigerate until ready to serve.

# Mary's Persimmon Pudding

When my friend Mary Townsley was 5 years old, she moved with her family from Virginia to southern Indiana. They were surprised to find that persimmons were so celebrated in Indiana that they were honored with a festival every September. Mary's recipe for persimmon pudding is rumored to be the very best, and I would agree.

### SERVES 8 TO 10

2 cups fresh persimmon pulp

2 cups sugar

3 large eggs

1 teaspoon baking soda

1½ cups buttermilk

1½ cups all-purpose flour

1 teaspoon baking powder

½ teaspoon ground cinnamon

¼ teaspoon salt

4 tablespoons salted butter

½ teaspoon vanilla extract

Whipped cream, for serving

Preheat the oven to 325°F. Combine the persimmon pulp, sugar, and eggs in a large bowl and beat until the ingredients are well incorporated. In another bowl, add the baking soda to the buttermilk and mix well. Then add the buttermilk mixture to the pulp mixture and blend. In a separate bowl, mix together the flour, baking powder, cinnamon, and salt. Add the dry ingredients to the wet ingredients and mix well.

Melt the butter in a 13 by 9-inch baking dish by placing in the preheated oven for 4 to 5 minutes. Transfer most of the butter to the persimmon mixture, leaving a little to coat the baking dish. Add the vanilla and mix well. Then pour the persimmon mixture into the prepared baking dish. Bake for 45 to 50 minutes, until set. Serve warm or cold, topped with whipped cream.

PERSIMMONS

# Chocolate Ganache

This is a beautiful way to finish off cakes, brownies, or ice cream. It's especially nice drizzled over angel food cake for a lighter dessert option.

**MAKES 1 CUP**

1½ cups semisweet chocolate chips

½ cup heavy cream or half-and-half

Place a few cups of water in the bottom of a double boiler. Bring the water to a boil, and then decrease the heat to medium. Add the chocolate chips and cream to the top of the double boiler. Stir to combine until smooth and creamy. Remove from the heat and garnish desserts as desired, or store in the refrigerator until ready to use. If stored in the refrigerator, bring it back to room temperature by warming it in the microwave on high power for 20 to 25 seconds; stir before using.

# To Age

The downsized empty nester that is me decided today that I must clean and organize the attic. This space over our garage became the resting place for all things that would not fit in the condo after our move from a larger home. It's not that these stored things aren't important parts of our lives—some of them really are—but I just can't find room for them inside this new, smaller dwelling. So today I'll try to sift through it all and see if it's possible to part the precious from the excess.

I make the climb up the steps and am overwhelmed by the sight of a collection of random boxes and plastic storage containers, scattered helter-skelter, filled with who knows what. We have carried these things at least three different times in the past two years from one storage location to another, and with each move, I'm more and more removed from the logic I used in packing them. What is all this stuff? And to make matters worse, it seems that each time one of us has gone in search of some stored thing, we've made an even bigger mess of the space. At the present time, there is not even an aisle to be found to plow through.

This will not make sense to most, but the next thing I do is turn on my heels and make my way back to my office to print out pretty labels in cheerful fonts. This is how I find the will to carry on in the ordering process ahead of me. Even though the labels state the boring truth ("extra bed linens," "Christmas decorations," "art supplies," and so forth), at least adding this creative step to the task at hand inspires me.

Hours later, a beautiful U-shaped path parades around the attic with rows of stuff tidily lined up against three walls. I've been distracted countless times in the process, since with each box I open, memories come bouncing out like a jack-in-the-box. I find myself wanting to go back and "do it again"—experience those days and months and years—only of course, this time I'd do it better and appreciate it more.

As I flip off the light and walk down the steps, I realize that now that the kids are off on their own grown-up adventures, there is no one here to appreciate the new orderliness of our lives packed away up there. The irony of this late-learned lesson is not lost on me, and I lean into the kind of smile that only comes with age.

**AGE: to let food get older under controlled conditions in order to improve flavor or texture or both.**

This AND That

# Jan's Hot Chocolate Mix

My friend Janice Manley shares this recipe with us. I'm sipping a steaming cup as I write and thinking about how I could send batches of this off to some of the college students I know. You may add Cinnamon Whipped Cream (page 141) for an even richer treat.

**MAKES ABOUT EIGHTEEN 1-CUP SERVINGS**

Sift all of the ingredients together in a large bowl and then transfer to a lidded container. Store in a cool, dry place for up to 3 months.

When ready to serve, add ¼ cup of the mix to 1 cup hot water and stir to dissolve.

½ cup cocoa
1 cup sugar
3 cups nonfat dry milk
dash of salt

# Peppermint Stick Iced Tea

It was a Sunday afternoon in December, bitter cold outside, and I had just awakened from a short nap. I'm not usually a napper, but I curled up on the sofa with a big blanket and the next thing I knew I was dreaming, not of sugarplums dancing in my head, but of iced tea brewed with crushed peppermint sticks. I recently made some dark chocolate peppermint bark for holiday gift giving, and I had about half a cup of crushed peppermint sticks left over. And so my afternoon dream was the inspiration for this iced tea. If you like your tea lightly sweetened with a hint of mint, you'll love this. I think it would be as refreshing in July as it is on a cold day.

### MAKES ABOUT 8 CUPS

4 cups water

½ cup crushed peppermint candy sticks

4 individual black tea bags or 2 family-size black tea bags

3 cups ice cubes, plus more for serving

Place the water in a saucepan and bring it to a boil over high heat. Add the peppermint to the boiling water and decrease the heat to medium. Stir to keep the peppermint from sticking to the bottom of the pan. Simmer for 3 to 5 minutes, stirring occasionally. Remove from the heat and add the tea bags. Cover the pan and allow the tea to brew for about 5 minutes. (If you have an ice tea maker with a compartment for sugar, you can place the crushed peppermint in this compartment and make your ice tea in the usual fashion.)

Pour the tea over the ice cubes in a heatproof pitcher. When ready to serve, strain the tea and any peppermint that didn't dissolve through a wire mesh strainer into a serving pitcher. Serve over ice.

# Carol's Coffee Punch

I'm not a coffee drinker. But when Carol Zimmer sent this recipe I knew it would be good, so I asked another trusted cook, Dee Stoelting, to test it for me. So, thank you to both of these ladies for bringing this punch recipe to you! Carol says this resembles a Frappuccino drink in flavor. Dee thought setting out whipped cream and caramel topping for the guests to garnish their individual servings would be fun.

**SERVES ABOUT 40**

1 gallon vanilla ice cream, softened

1 gallon chocolate ice cream, softened

1¼ cups instant coffee granules

5 cups boiling water

2½ cups sugar

1 gallon milk

Whipped cream, for garnish

Caramel ice cream topping, for garnish

Place both ice creams in a large punch bowl. In a separate large bowl, mix the coffee, water, and sugar to dissolve. Pour the coffee mixture over the ice cream and stir to melt. Add the milk and mix well. Serve cool, garnished with whipped cream and caramel ice cream topping.

# Simple Syrup

Keep a container of this in your refrigerator during the spring and summer to mix up a quick batch of lemonade, sweet tea, or iced coffee. It keeps indefinitely.

**MAKES ABOUT 8 CUPS**

5 cups water

5 cups sugar

Bring the water to a boil in a large saucepan. Add the sugar and stir until completely dissolved. Remove from the heat. Cool and store in a covered container in the refrigerator.

# Raspberry Lemonade

I love serving this lemonade at parties. It's so festive and refreshing. Rather than purchasing expensive bottles of simple syrup, make your own. If you're serving the lemonade from a pitcher, add fresh lemon slices and whole raspberries to the pitcher for a nice flair. However, if serving the lemonade from a decanter that has a spigot, refrain from any floating garnishes, since they have a tendency to get stuck in the spigot and impede the flow.

**MAKES ABOUT THIRTY
10-OUNCE SERVINGS**

5 quarts cold water

6 cups lemon juice, either freshly squeezed or bottled

5 cups Simple Syrup (page 137)

12 ounces frozen raspberries, pureed and strained to remove seeds

4 cups ice cubes

2 lemons, thinly sliced, for garnish

Fresh whole raspberries, for garnish

In a large container, combine the water, lemon juice, Simple Syrup, pureed raspberries, and ice cubes and mix until the pureed raspberries are fully distributed. Store in the refrigerator until ready to serve (for up to 10 days). Add the garnishes to each serving.

# fresh fruit shake

This recipe will provide you with a refreshing beverage for any time of the day, at any time of the year. It's a great "portable" way to make sure you get a maximum number of nutrients with a minimum amount of effort. Cheers!

## SERVES 1

1 cup freshly squeezed orange juice

1 banana, sliced

1 clementine, peeled and sectioned

10 strawberries, stemmed

4 ice cubes

Place the juice and the fruit in a blender and mix well. Add the ice cubes and blend a few seconds longer to chop the ice. Serve immediately.

# Janet's Tarragon Vinaigrette

This recipe is from my friend Janet Baker. It comes together quickly and tastes so fresh. You may use this dressing on both lettuce salads and pasta salads.

**MAKES 1 CUP**

½ cup vegetable oil

¼ cup tarragon vinegar

¼ cup sugar

1 teaspoon salt

½ teaspoon Tabasco sauce

Pinch of freshly ground black pepper

Whisk the oil, vinegar, sugar, salt, Tabasco, and pepper together in a bowl. Pour into a bottle and store in the refrigerator for up to 2 weeks.

**140**

# Cinnamon Whipped Cream

It's surprising how many different desserts are improved considerably by garnishing them with this simple version of whipped cream. It's also wonderful on hot cocoa.

**MAKES ABOUT 2 CUPS**

1½ cups heavy whipping cream

¼ cup powdered sugar

½ teaspoon ground cinnamon

In the bowl of an electric mixer fitted with a whip attachment, whip the cream on high speed until it forms soft peaks. Add the powdered sugar and cinnamon and mix just until incorporated. Store in the refrigerator for up to 2 days in a covered container.

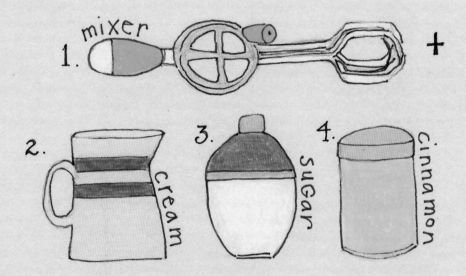

# HOUR POWER Whipped Cream

I gave this whipped cream this goofy name to illustrate its staying power. Whipped cream has a tendency to fall flat after sitting out for a while. By adding the powdered sugar, the whipped cream becomes a little more stable and can survive at room temperature for up to an hour. I've used this topping on desserts that will be sitting out on a buffet table, which helps to relieve my worries about it "melting" before guests can enjoy the final course.

## MAKES ABOUT 2½ CUPS

2 cups heavy cream

½ teaspoon vanilla extract

¾ cup powdered sugar

In the bowl of an electric mixer fitted with a whip attachment, beat the cream on high speed until it thickens. Add the vanilla and incorporate into the cream. Gradually add the powdered sugar and beat until it forms soft peaks. Be careful not to overbeat. Store in the refrigerator for up to 2 days, until ready to serve.

# Salt & Pepper Tortilla Strips

In less than 15 minutes you can add such a festive garnish to any Mexican salad or soup. These strips are more affordable than the store-bought variety, and since they are baked rather than fried, they are a healthier option as well. I like to package these in cellophane bags tied with a bright ribbon. Team them up with chili ingredients in a basket to create a memorable gift. Seasoned salt and seasoned pepper can be found in the spice aisle of your grocery store.

### SERVES 16 AS A GARNISH OR TOPPING

1 (16-ounce) package extra-thin yellow corn tortillas

Vegetable oil cooking spray

Seasoned salt

Seasoned pepper

Preheat the oven to 425°F. Line a large baking sheet with parchment paper. Coat the parchment paper with cooking spray. Using kitchen shears, cut the tortillas into long, thin strips, about ¼ inch wide. Scatter the strips evenly over the prepared baking sheet. Spray the strips with vegetable oil cooking spray and season with the salt and pepper. Bake for 5 minutes.

Remove from the oven and turn the strips with a spatula. Spray with the cooking spray once again and return to the oven. Bake for an additional 4 to 5 minutes, until golden brown. Serve warm or at room temperature. If packaging, let cool completely before placing in bags or storage containers for up to 1 week.

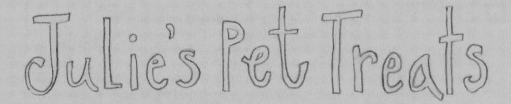

# Julie's Pet Treats

My beautiful niece, Julie Roberts, recently finished her vet tech degree,
and for her graduation gift I decided to fill a big jar to the brim with
these treats so that she can begin spoiling all her patients.

### MAKES ABOUT 36 TREATS

2 cups whole wheat flour

1 cup yellow cornmeal

1 teaspoon salt

2 chicken bouillon cubes

1 cup hot water

⅓ cup vegetable oil

1 large egg

Preheat the oven to 350°F. Line a baking sheet with parchment paper.

In the bowl of an electric mixer using a paddle attachment, stir together the
whole wheat flour, cornmeal, and salt. Dissolve the bouillon cubes in the hot
water, and stir to combine. Add the bouillon mixture, the oil, and egg to the
flour mixture and mix well. Roll a teaspoonful of the dough into a ball and
place on the prepared baking sheet. You may add a little more flour if the
dough is too sticky to handle. Flatten the ball of dough slightly. Repeat with
the rest of the dough.

Bake for 20 to 25 minutes, until lightly browned and firm. Cool completely
before serving to your pet. Store in an airtight container for up to 1 month.

# Stir

Just yesterday I listened as a friend of mine shared some very interesting facts about a bird found on the coasts of Scandinavia, Iceland, and Greenland. It is called the Guillemot and is penguin-like in appearance, slim with a pointed bill, dark head, and white breast. My friend explained that right before breeding season begins, in late May, these particular birds congregate on rocks and cliff ledges, packed tightly together in large colonies.

Ornithologists have studied these birds for a very long time and have noted some specific behaviors common to the Guillemots. After breeding, a single egg is laid directly onto the bare rock of a narrow ledge, often right next to dozens of other single eggs laid in the same fashion. The eggs all look the same to us, but somehow each parent knows its own particular egg. And if that egg is moved even a fraction of an inch, the male and female parents (who take turns to incubate the egg) notice from afar and fly back to the egg to reposition it, ensuring its safety on the narrow ledge.

There was just something so reassuring, so comforting about this to me. I thought that if this bird could be so attentive to the slightest movement of its single egg, how much more would my Creator sense when I was "moved." Whether I was stirred by the joy of a moment or through despair, would not my Creator fly to my side and say, "I see where you are . . . Tell me everything."

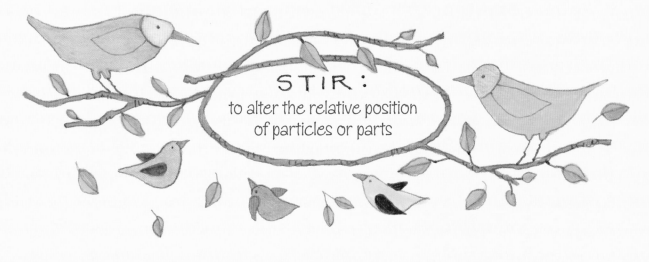

STIR:
to alter the relative position
of particles or parts

# SUBSTITUTIONS

| INGREDIENT | QUANTITY | SUBSTITUTE |
|---|---|---|
| Baking powder | 1 teaspoon | ¼ teaspoon baking soda plus ½ teaspoon cream of tartar |
| Chocolate | 1 square (1 ounce) | 3 tablespoons cocoa powder plus 1 tablespoon butter |
| Cornstarch | 1 tablespoon | 2 tablespoons all-purpose flour |
| Cracker crumbs | ¾ cup | 1 cup bread crumbs |
| Dry mustard | 1 teaspoon | 1 tablespoon prepared mustard |
| Flour, self-rising | 1 cup | 1 cup all-purpose flour, ½ teaspoon salt, and 1 teaspoon baking powder |
| Herbs, fresh | 1 tablespoon | 1 teaspoon dried herbs |
| Milk, whole | 1 cup | ½ cup evaporated milk plus ½ cup water |
| Onion, fresh | 1 small | 1 tablespoon instant minced onion, rehydrated |
| Sugar, brown | ½ cup | 2 tablespoons molasses in ½ cup granulated sugar |
| Sugar, powdered | 1 cup | 1 cup granulated sugar plus 1 teaspoon cornstarch |
| Tomato juice | 1 cup | ½ cup tomato sauce plus ½ cup water |

# Metric Conversions and Equivalents

## APPROXIMATE METRIC EQUIVALENTS

### Weight

| | | | |
|---|---|---|---|
| ¼ ounce | 7 grams | 3 ounces | 85 grams |
| ½ ounce | 14 grams | 4 ounces (¼ pound) | 113 grams |
| ¾ ounce | 21 grams | 5 ounces | 142 grams |
| 1 ounce | 28 grams | 6 ounces | 170 grams |
| 1¼ ounces | 35 grams | 7 ounces | 198 grams |
| 1½ ounces | 42.5 grams | 8 ounces (½ pound) | 227 grams |
| 1⅔ ounces | 45 grams | 16 ounces (1 pound) | 454 grams |
| 2 ounces | 57 grams | 35¼ ounces (2.2 pounds) | 1 kilogram |

### Volume

| | | | |
|---|---|---|---|
| ¼ teaspoon | 1 milliliter | ½ cup (4 fluid ounces) | 120 milliliters |
| ½ teaspoon | 2.5 milliliters | ⅔ cup | 160 milliliters |
| ¾ teaspoon | 4 milliliters | ¾ cup | 180 milliliters |
| 1 teaspoon | 5 milliliters | 1 cup (8 fluid ounces) | 240 milliliters |
| 1¼ teaspoons | 6 milliliters | 1¼ cups | 300 milliliters |
| 1½ teaspoons | 7.5 milliliters | 1½ cups (12 fluid ounces) | 360 milliliters |
| 1¾ teaspoons | 8.5 milliliters | 1⅔ cups | 400 milliliters |
| 2 teaspoons | 10 milliliters | 2 cups (1 pint) | 460 milliliters |
| 1 tablespoon (½ fluid ounce) | 15 milliliters | 4 cups (1 quart) | 0.95 liter |
| 2 tablespoons (1 fluid ounce) | 30 milliliters | 1 quart plus ¼ cup | 1 liter |
| ¼ cup | 60 milliliters | 4 quarts (1 gallon) | 3.8 liters |
| ⅓ cup | 80 milliliters | | |

### Length

| | | | |
|---|---|---|---|
| ⅛ inch | 3 millimeters | 2 inches | 5 centimeters |
| ¼ inch | 6 millimeters | 4 inches | 10 centimeters |
| ½ inch | 1.25 centimeters | 6 inches | 15¼ centimeters |
| 1 inch | 2.5 centimeters | 12 inches (1 foot) | 30 centimeters |

## METRIC CONVERSION FORMULAS

| To Convert | Multiply |
|---|---|
| Ounces to grams | Ounces by 28.35 |
| Pounds to kilograms | Pounds by 0.454 |
| Teaspoons to milliliters | Teaspoons by 4.93 |
| Tablespoons to milliliters | Tablespoons by 14.79 |
| Fluid ounces to milliliters | Fluid ounces by 29.57 |
| Cups to milliliters | Cups by 236.59 |
| Cups to liters | Cups by 0.236 |
| Pints to liters | Pints by 0.473 |
| Quarts to liters | Quarts by 0.946 |
| Inches to centimeters | Inches by 2.54 |

## COMMON INGREDIENTS AND THEIR APPROXIMATE EQUIVALENTS

1 cup all-purpose flour = 140 grams

1 stick butter (4 ounces • ½ cup • 8 tablespoons) = 110 grams

1 cup butter (8 ounces • 2 sticks • 16 tablespoons) = 220 grams

1 cup brown sugar, firmly packed = 225 grams

1 cup granulated sugar = 200 grams

## OVEN TEMPERATURES

To convert Fahrenheit to Celsius, subtract 32 from Fahrenheit, multiply the result by 5, then divide by 9.

| Description | Fahrenheit | Celsius | British Gas Mark |
|---|---|---|---|
| Very cool | 200° | 95° | 0 |
| Very cool | 225° | 110° | ¼ |
| Very cool | 250° | 120° | ½ |
| Cool | 275° | 135° | 1 |
| Cool | 300° | 150° | 2 |
| Warm | 325° | 165° | 3 |
| Moderate | 350° | 175° | 4 |
| Moderately hot | 375° | 190° | 5 |
| Fairly hot | 400° | 200° | 6 |
| Hot | 425° | 220° | 7 |
| Very hot | 450° | 230° | 8 |
| Very hot | 475° | 245° | 9 |

Information compiled from a variety of sources, including *Recipes into Type* by Joan Whitman and Dolores Simon (Newton, MA: Biscuit Books, 2000); *The New Food Lover's Companion* by Sharon Tyler Herbst (Hauppauge, NY: Barron's, 1995); and *Rosemary Brown's Big Kitchen Instruction Book* (Kansas City, MO: Andrews McMeel, 1998).

# Index